WRITTEN BY
CHANTAL HENRY-BIABAUD, DORINE BARBEY,
MARTINE BECK, ROGER DIÉVART

COVER DESIGN BY
STEPHANIE BLUMENTHAL

TRANSLATED AND ADAPTED BY
PAULA SCHANILEC AND ROSEMARY WALLNER

PUBLISHED BY CREATIVE EDUCATION
123 South Broad Street, Mankato, Minnesota 56001
Creative Education is an imprint of The Creative Company

Library of Congress Cataloging-in-Publication Data
[Decouvrir notre corps. English]
The human body / by Chantal Henry-Biabaud et al. ; [translated and adapted by Paula Schanilec].
(Creative discoveries)
Includes index.
Summary: Describes the human body, all its organs and systems,
and things people can do to keep their bodies healthy.
ISBN: 0-88682-951-8
1. Body, Human—Juvenile literature.   [1. Body, Human.]
I. Henry-Biabaud, Chantal.   II. Title   III. Series
QP37.H39513   1999
612—dc21   97-23927

First edition

2 4 6 8 9 7 5 3 1

THE HUMAN BODY

CONTENTS

CREATIVE EDUCATION

Short or tall; heavy or light; young or old; blond, red-headed, brown, or black; fair- or dark-skinned; the basic model is the same.

We each have a head with hair, two eyes, two ears, a nose, a mouth; a body with two arms and two legs; and a spine to keep us upright.

We are all made this way because we all belong to the same species. We are human beings, or to be technical, *Homo sapiens.*

The human species is part of the larger animal kingdom. We are distinguished from other animals by our large and highly developed brains, our use of language, and our upright posture.

Your birthday is your own special day, because it is the date when you were born.
Human babies start out as a tiny egg cell inside their mother. The egg cell grows larger and larger in the mother's womb, making her abdomen larger and larger. This time is called pregnancy. After nine months, the cell has grown into a baby that is ready to be born.

There are 250 babies being born somewhere in the world at every minute of the day and night. Each baby has a father and a mother who also were born in the same way. Like human babies, every animal has a father and a mother as well.

Not all animals are born in the same way.
Some hatch out of an egg the mother lays. Inside the egg is food for the young animal, so it can grow protected inside its shell. All birds lay eggs, and so do fish, insects, and most reptiles. Tortoise and turtle eggs are round, not oval, like most birds' eggs, and they have a soft shell.

Once the mother tortoise has laid her eggs, she leaves and doesn't look after them. A baby tortoise has just hatched.

Ladybugs and other insects lay many tiny, fragile eggs. They have to lay so many because only a few survive until they hatch.

A mother ladybug lays her eggs after the father fertilizes them.

All baby mammals grow inside their mother, just as human babies do. Have you ever seen puppies or kittens drinking milk from their mother? All animals that spend their early days suckling milk from their mothers are called mammals, including humans. Mammals have a few other things in common too. They are all warm-blooded, and they all have hair.

When a man and a woman love each other, they often want to share their love by having children. Each has inside them half of what is needed to make a baby: a man has the sperm, and a woman has the ovum.

Sperm   Ovum

Conception (fertilization) happens when the sperm and ovum meet. When one sperm and one ovum join together inside the mother, the new cell divides, increasing in size, and grows into a baby.

A man's chromosome decides if the baby will be a girl or a boy. Inside the woman's ovum, the chromosome that decides the baby's sex is always in the shape of an X. In the sperm, it is sometimes X-shaped, and sometimes Y-shaped. If a sperm with an X

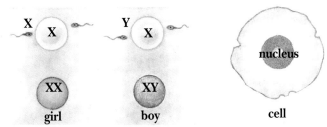

X — X   Y — X   nucleus

XX   XY   cell
girl   boy

chromosome joins the ovum, they will produce an XX cell and the baby will be a girl. If the ovum meets a Y chromosome, they will produce an XY cell and the baby will be a boy.

Red   Chestnut   Black

Hair can be all sorts of different colors.

Light brown   Ash blond   Golden

Chromosomes are made up of genes.

Everyone has two sets of genes, one from the father and one from the mother. Genes carry all the instructions to make a new baby. There are genes for everything: the color of the baby's skin, her eyes, her hair, her height, and the shape of her ears. You probably look like your mother in some ways and your father in others. That is because you are a mixture of genes from both of them.

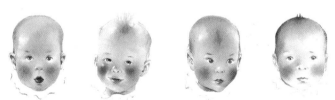

As soon as an egg cell is fertilized, the characteristics of the new baby are there.

That means that you inherited your mother's eyes or your father's height about nine months before you were born! Your parents received their genes from their parents, who got them from theirs, and so on. No two people ever receive the same exact genes, though, and so no two people in the world are exactly alike.

What about twins?

Sometimes, the mother produces two ova. If two sperms fertilize two eggs, two babies will start to develop at the same time. They won't be identical twins—one might be a boy, the other a girl.

Sometimes, the fertilized ovum divides into two, and the two parts form identical twins. They are always the same sex, and they look alike. A mother can have three, four, five, or even six babies at the same time—but that is very unusual.

The egg develops inside the uterus, which is also called the womb. The muscles of the uterus stretch to give the baby room to grow. Attached to the uterus is the placenta. This is where the baby's blood meets with the mother's blood.

The link between mother and baby

Inside the uterus, the baby lies cradled in a bag of watery fluid, called amniotic fluid. This fluid protects it from bumps as its mother moves around. The umbilical cord connects the baby to the placenta, a kind of sac. It goes from the baby's belly, through the watery fluid, and into the placenta.

At one month, the egg is the size of a pea. At this stage, it is called an embryo. The heart begins to beat at six weeks old.

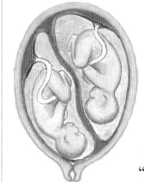

Identical twins grow in the same bag of fluid and share the same placenta.

How does the baby eat while inside the mother? Blood passes through the placenta and along the umbilical cord. The blood carries nutrients, water, and oxygen to the embryo and takes away waste matter. A woman expecting a baby gets more tired than she did before she was pregnant because of the extra work her body is doing.

How does the embryo grow inside the mother? At two months, the embryo has grown to the size of a walnut. The head and limbs start to appear. The embryo has the beginnings of fingers and toes. Outlines appear where the ears will be, and eyelids cover the eyes.

Non-identical, or fraternal, twins grow in separate bags, and each has its own placenta.

At three months the embryo begins to look like a miniature baby. It is now called a fetus (pronounced "fee-tus"). The fetus is three inches (7.6 cm) long and is starting to swallow and move.

At four months the fetus sleeps a lot during the day as the mother moves around. Then in the evening, when she relaxes, the fetus wakes up and begins to move its head, arms, and legs.

At five months the mother can feel the fetus moving. It kicks and turns somersaults, trying to find the most comfortable position. Its hair begins to grow. It can swallow some of the fluid that surrounds it, wiggle its fingers, and suck its thumb.

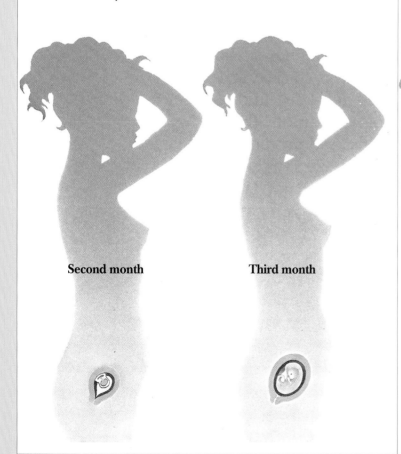

Second month   Third month

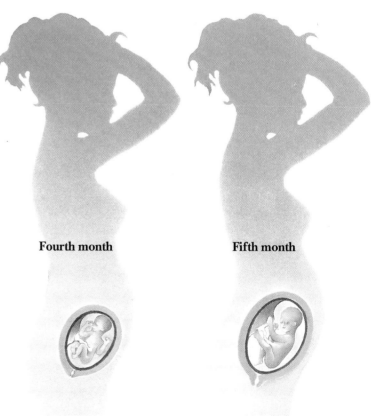

Fourth month   Fifth month

At six months of pregnancy, the fetus weighs two pounds (0.9 kg). When it drinks too much, it gets hiccups, which makes the mother's belly jump. It can urinate, and it has fingernails. Its skin, which was fine and delicate, is now growing stronger. The fetus is getting bigger and curling into a ball, because there isn't enough space to stretch out anymore. It can hear sounds—the fluid around the fetus muffles some sounds but a piercing cry can make it jump.

At seven months it opens its eyes. It can hear the sounds made by the mother's body—the beating of her heart, the sound of her voice. It's moving a lot now, kicking and punching in its cramped quarters.

At eight months it has grown so big that it can't turn somersaults inside its mother anymore. The tiny tongue is able to taste. Everything is finished. All the fetus needs is to gain a bit more weight. Its head is usually pointing downward, ready to be born at nine months.

At nine months, the fetus weighs about seven pounds (3 kg). It is usually born after nine months in the uterus, but sometimes it is born earlier. A baby born before the eighth month is called a premature baby. It has not had time to finish growing and is weak and delicate. Its lungs are not fully developed. Premature babies are put into incubators—small heated cots where doctors and nurses can look after them.

1. Fetus 2. Placenta 3. Bag of amniotic fluid
4. Inside the uterus 5. Umbilical cord

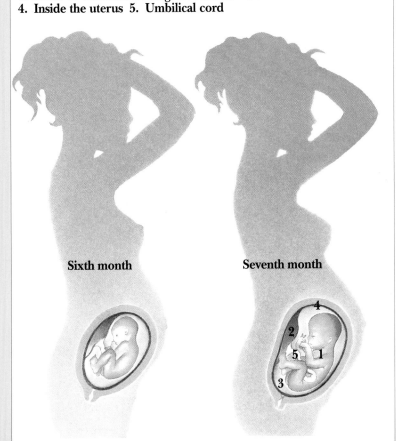

Sixth month   Seventh month

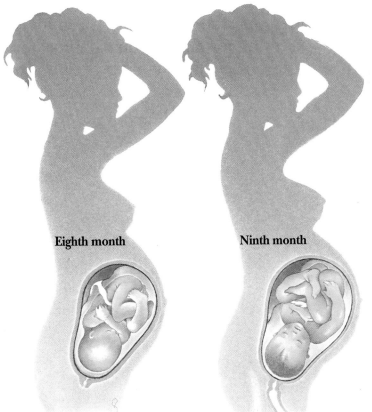

Eighth month   Ninth month

The time comes for the baby to be born. The mother knows when she is going to give birth. She starts to get pains in her abdomen as her muscles contract to push the baby toward the opening of the uterus. Delivering a baby is called "labor" because birth is hard work for mother and baby.

After several hours of labor, the baby comes out through the mother's vagina, which stretches to allow the baby to be born. Usually, the head appears first, followed by the rest of the body. The placenta, or afterbirth, follows about 20 minutes later.

Birth must be quite a shock for the baby. For nine months, he has been in the dark in a warm liquid, and suddenly there is light and noise. He begins to cry, a sign that he is breathing well.

The umbilical cord is no longer needed; it can be cut without hurting mother or child. If held up, a newborn baby can move his legs as if trying to walk. When a baby is born in a hospital, matching name bracelets are strapped on his wrist and his mother's wrist.

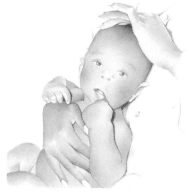

Babies have a space between the bones of their skulls called the fontanel.

Her umbilical cord will dry up and drop off soon after birth.

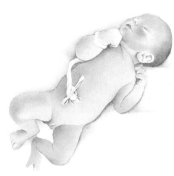

Although a newborn baby is tiny, he is large in the lives of his parents from the moment he is born. One of the first things the parents do is give their new child a name.

Do you have one first name or several? Do you know why your parents chose your name?

Customs vary, depending on the nationality and culture to which you belong. In Thailand, every baby is called Nou, meaning "little mouse" until he is one month old. Then a name is chosen for him according to the day on which he was born. In Kashmir, children are not given their own names until they are four or five years old.

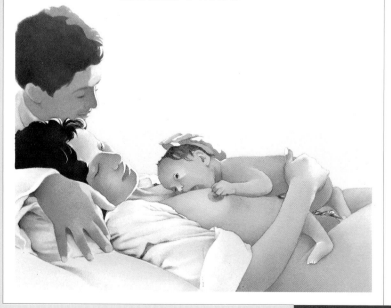

As soon as a baby is born, he is able to suck milk from his mother's nipple.

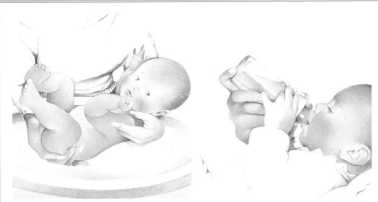

Babies love baths . . .

. . . and being fed.

Babies see best up close. They sleep much of the time.

A baby is often hungry. Before the baby was born, she was fed all the time, day and night, through the umbilical cord. Now, she lets her parents know she is hungry by crying. For the first weeks, she feeds every three to four hours, drinking milk from her mother's breast or from a bottle. Gradually, the parents give her something other than milk, and the baby can wait longer between feeding times.

A baby loves to be cuddled by her parents or an older brother or sister. She likes the warm feeling and smell of people who love her and people she knows best. She learns about the outside world through contact with them. Loud noises and sudden move-

ments frighten her. A baby can't see very well at first. She is only able to see shapes and bright colors.

When the remains of the umbilical cord drop off, a small scar is left—the belly button, or navel.

A baby must gain weight. At first doctors and nurses weigh her frequently to make sure she is growing properly. She gains about one ounce (28 g) a day for the first two months. After awhile, she is weighed every few months or so. A baby should gain weight quickly. If she is not gaining weight or if she loses weight, that may be a sign that she is not well.

Japan

Papua-
New Guinea

Mothers all over the world choose different ways to carry their babies.

Laos

Africa

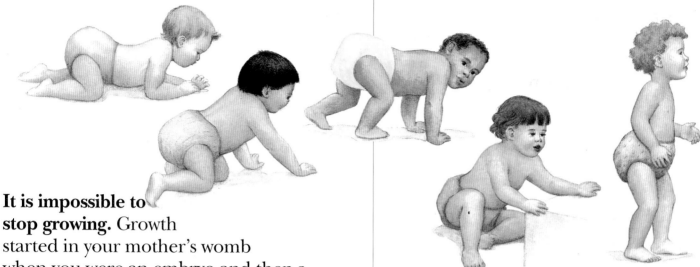

It is impossible to stop growing. Growth started in your mother's womb when you were an embryo and then a fetus. A newborn baby grows bigger, turns into a child, then an adolescent, and finally into an adult.

When you are young, you grow very fast. Shoes that were bought just a couple of months ago get tight, and last winter's pants are much too small now. Ever since the first cell divided, long before you were born, the cells of your body have been multiplying, forming new tissues.

Your body's tissues are grouped together to make up different organs.

Every part of your body is made up of cells. There are many different kinds of cells, and each kind has a special job to do. In the center of each cell is the nucleus. This is where the chromosomes are.

Your cells are changing all the time. Those that are too old are replaced with new ones. New cells are made when one cell divides and the nucleus splits in two.

In the first weeks of life, you grow in weight and length. Then you start to learn different things: Your senses develop and your bones get harder and stronger. Every organ and every part of your body has a timetable of growth. There may be times when your feet seem too big for the rest of you, or your mouth seems crowded with teeth that are too large. This is normal. Your body will work itself out in the end.

The big change into adulthood: adolescence
During these years, a boy becomes a man, and a girl becomes a woman, capable of having children of their own.

Hormones are the body's chemical messengers. Glands release hormones into the blood. Hormones from the pituitary gland control growth. They are especially hard at work during puberty. Puberty is the growth stage between childhood and adulthood. It is the time when your body changes and matures to become capable of sexual reproduction, making babies. This change happens during preadolescence and adolescence, between the ages of 10 and 16 for girls, and around 12 to 14 for boys.

During puberty, you feel many strong emotions—your personality grows along with your body, and you become more independent. But you might be uncomfortable in a body that is changing so much. Parents and teenagers can become frustrated with each other. Both are adjusting to the changes.

A strong, healthy body must be fed in many different ways. A balanced diet and plenty of exercise are vital for a strong, healthy body—but many other things are important for health too. Fun, learning, and the love and attention of family and friends help to build a healthy mind and body.

Adults have finished growing. Between the ages of 20 and 30, the body is at its strongest and the brain at its most alert. As you get older, your cells renew themselves more slowly, so it takes longer to repair damaged or diseased parts of the body. Finally, like the worn-out engine of an old car, your heart stops, and you die. But life goes on, as children grow up, get married, and have babies of their own.

Your body has different systems that work to keep you going. The system that deals with food and waste is called the digestive system. **The digestive system breaks down the food and drink you swallow** into tiny particles that pass into the bloodstream and give you energy.

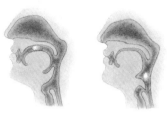

When you swallow, the epiglottis shuts off the opening to your windpipe like a lid, so that food doesn't go down into your lungs.

Your digestive system is like a long tube, which begins at your mouth and ends at your anus. In an adult, that tube is about 30 feet (9 m) long, and most of it is coiled up in the abdomen.

How does the digestive system work?
Digestion starts with a mouthful of food that is chewed and mixed with saliva until it is soft and mushy. When you swallow, the food goes down the esophagus to your stomach. There, acidic digestive juices dilute the food into a thick, soupy liquid. Muscles squeeze the food along a little at a time into the small intestine, where useful particles of food called nutrients are separated from the indigestible waste. Nutrients pass into the bloodstream across the lining of the small intestine on their way to feed the body's cells. Undigested waste continues on through the large intestine and leaves the body as feces or urine when people go to the toilet.

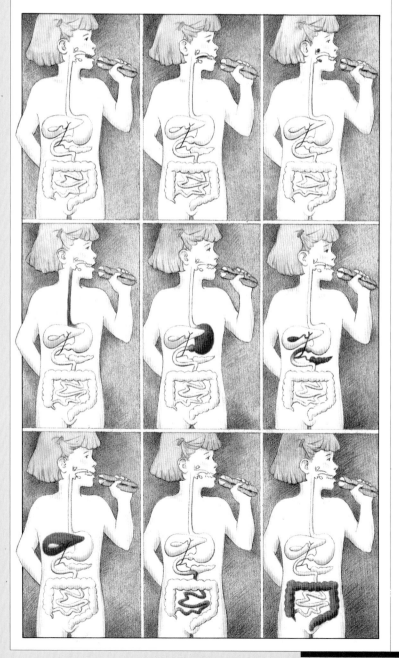

Esophagus
Liver
Stomach
Small intestine
Large intestine
Appendix
Anus

Digestive system seen from the front

Most of the nutrients that pass into the bloodstream go to the liver before traveling to the rest of the body. The liver works like a factory, processing nutrients to feed the cells and storing vitamins. The kidneys clean the blood and turn any waste into urine.

The liver produces a liquid called bile, which is used in the small intestine to help digest fats.

The digestive system is complicated, so there is more than one reason why you sometimes get a stomachache. If you have eaten too much, you may feel sick. That's a form of indigestion. If you have swallowed germs or eaten something that isn't fresh, you may get food poisoning. Your stomach won't accept the food—instead, the muscles of the stomach contract strongly and send the food gushing back upward, making you vomit. If your intestine reacts as well, contracting rapidly to get rid of the bad food, you have diarrhea.

People with "heartburn" are in fact having trouble with their stomach. They probably have indigestion.

A virus can make you ill with gastroenteritis. You may also get a stomachache if you are nervous or annoyed. If you don't eat enough fiber and drink enough water, you may become constipated, which can be painful. Whole grain bread, prunes, or high-fiber cereal should take care of your system.

Appendicitis
If the tiny appendix at the bottom of your large intestine becomes infected, you develop a bad pain in your abdomen. A doctor will need to remove the infected appendix during surgery.

Unwanted visitors
Occasionally, people get worms in their stomach or intestines. A special medicine will get rid of them quickly. People who have worms must keep their nails short, because the worms' eggs can lodge underneath when the person scratches their skin, and then the worms might be passed on to others.

Teeth not only look nice but are useful too. They bite, chew, nibble, munch, crunch, tear, grind, gnaw—just try eating without them.

Animals use their teeth for many things—even for carrying their young.

Teeth are different shapes for doing different jobs. The incisors at the front cut like a chisel. Next come the canine teeth— they're pointed, good for tearing up food. The big, flat teeth at the back are molars. You use them to chew your food.

Your mouth is like a cave. The roof of your mouth is called the palate, and at the far, dark end there's the uvula. Your tongue rolls your food around and then sends it down your throat.

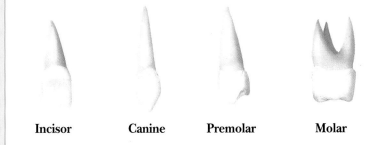

Incisor   Canine   Premolar   Molar

Teeth are living things. They may not look like it, but they are in fact small bones.

Teeth are embedded into the jawbones. The upper jaw does not move; the lower jaw can move up and down and from side to side.

What is a tooth made of? What you see is the shiny white enamel that protects your teeth from breaking easily and from heat and cold, as well as from all the germs that live in your mouth.

The dentine underneath protects the pulp, a soft tissue holding blood vessels that feed the tooth and nerves. Have you ever had a toothache? It's the nerves in the root of the tooth that make you feel the pain.

Just like a tree, with its roots in the soil, a tooth has its roots in the gum and is firmly embedded in the jawbone. The part above the gum is called the crown. The part of the tooth you can't see is called the root.

Mouth

You use the incisors at the front of your mouth when you bite into an apple.

All these things are good for your teeth: water containing fluoride, fish, milk, butter, cheese, and eggs, which contain calcium— a mineral that keeps your teeth strong. Fresh fruit and green vegetables contain vitamin C to give you healthy gums.

1. Enamel 2. Dentine 3. Pulp 4. Blood vessels 5. Nerves

Primary teeth and permanent teeth

First teeth

Babies don't usually have any teeth when they are born. Some say that King Louis XIV of France was born with a tooth. But that's rare.

When a baby is about six months old, his cheeks look red, and he cries and drools a lot. Then a first tooth appears: a lower incisor—the baby is "cutting teeth." It hurts because the teeth are cutting through the gum. The poor baby is grumpy and sometimes has a fever.

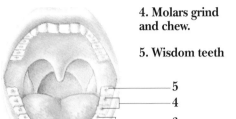

1. Incisors cut and slice.

2. Canines cut and tear.

3. Premolars grind and chew.

4. Molars grind and chew.

5. Wisdom teeth

The lower incisors are the first to appear, followed by the upper ones. Then come the canines, and then the molars.

At two and a half years old, a child has 20 teeth, sometimes called "milk teeth" because they appear during the time the baby is drinking a lot of milk. Later, between the ages of six and 11, these teeth fall out, pushed out of the way by the second set of teeth. It hardly hurts at all.

Teeth for life

Underneath each primary, or baby tooth, is another tooth waiting to grow and replace it.

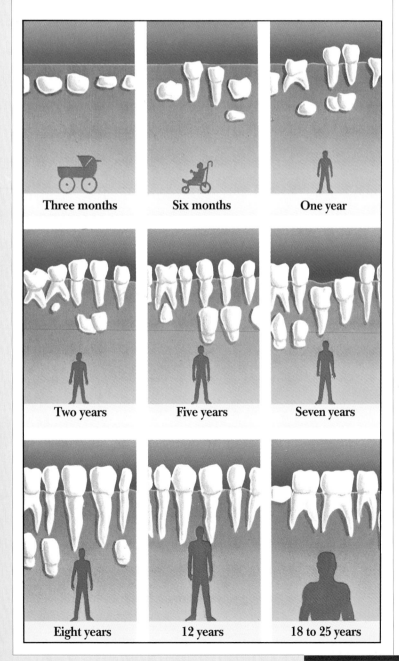

Three months | Six months | One year

Two years | Five years | Seven years

Eight years | 12 years | 18 to 25 years

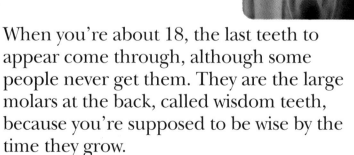

X-rays show what your eyes can't see: under the milk teeth are permanent teeth waiting to grow.

When you're about 18, the last teeth to appear come through, although some people never get them. They are the large molars at the back, called wisdom teeth, because you're supposed to be wise by the time they grow.

An adult has 32 teeth: eight incisors, four canines, eight premolars, and 12 molars.

A long time ago, people used their teeth more than you do today. Their teeth were very strong. They were used for crunching raw vegetables and tearing and biting raw meat. There were no sugary sweets to eat.

This is how a dentist fills a cavity.

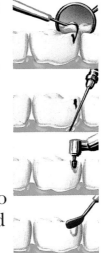

What would someone do if they had a toothache? There were no dentists. A person might try to help the pain with herbs, but if the pain became too bad, they could go to a traveling tooth-puller. He would yank the bad tooth out, and since there was no pain medicine, a musician would play to drown out the yells.

People should go to the dentist at least twice a year for a checkup. If a tooth becomes sensitive to cold or heat, go as soon as possible. You may have a small hole, or cavity. If infection gets into the pulp, it will hurt a lot.

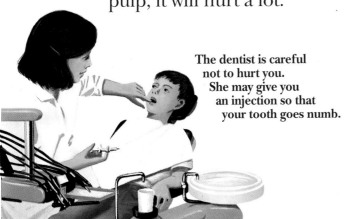

The dentist is careful not to hurt you. She may give you an injection so that your tooth goes numb.

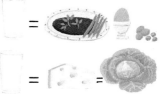

Which would you like best: a glass of milk, an ounce of cheese, or a large cabbage? All these contain the same amount of calcium.

How should you care for your teeth? Brush two to three teeth at a time in a circular motion, massaging the gums. Then rinse your mouth well. It's best to brush your teeth after every meal, but be sure to brush them after breakfast in the morning and before you go to bed at night. Then you will brush away food, which builds into plaque, as well as germs that could attack the dentine and damage it. Flossing at least once a day is important for cleaning between teeth, where most problems begin.

Your teeth, like your bones, grow until you are about 18 years old. What you eat will make a difference as to how strong your teeth are. Eat plenty of fresh vegetables; drink milk and eat cheese for their calcium.

Be careful about what you bite—your teeth aren't as strong as a squirrel's!

Biting thread and crunching candy are both bad for your teeth.

Sugar is the enemy of healthy teeth. When sugar mixes with saliva, the sugar turns into acid, which eats into the enamel and makes holes. It's fine to eat sweets occasionally, but always brush your teeth right after you have eaten or drunk anything sugary.

What are the best things to eat?

If you are going to grow up healthy, you need many different foods every day. You couldn't survive if you only ate or drank one thing, like a cookie or a soft drink. Scientists have shown that the meals you eat during one day should contain at least one food from each of the six groups. You should also drink eight to 10 glasses of water a day.

Meat, fish, eggs, and dairy products supply important nutrients for a growing body. These foods all contain proteins, which are

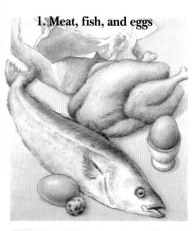
1. Meat, fish, and eggs

2. Bread, rice, cereal, and starch

3. Fruits and vegetables

vital for the healthy development of your body. Every living part of you needs proteins if it is to grow properly. Meat gives you iron for your blood and muscles. Fish gives you essential fatty acids and minerals like magnesium and phosphorus. Dairy products provide calcium for healthy bones. Vitamins are important while your body is growing and forming. There are many vitamins in fruits and vegetables. You should eat five servings of fruits and vegetables each day.

There is as much protein in a quart of milk as there is in a steak, four eggs, or three pounds (1.3 kg) of potatoes.

Carbohydrates fuel us. Foods such as bread, rice, cereal, corn, and potatoes are the building blocks of a balanced diet. They are rich in carbohydrates, which give your body needed energy.

Sugar provides a quick boost, but too much is unhealthy.

4. Dairy products

5. Fats

Animal and vegetable fats are harder to digest than carbohydrates but produce twice as much energy. Eat these sparingly.

Physical exercise uses up energy fast. If you are bicycling, you will need more food than if you are spending the afternoon watching television.

6. Sugar

Different people have different needs. We do not all need the same amount of food each day.

What good does good food do?

About 70 percent of your body is made up of water. That's why it is important to drink about a half gallon (2 l), or eight to 10 glasses, of water every day.

A good breakfast is an important start to the day. Perhaps you eat a cooked breakfast. Breakfast foods vary in different countries, but a healthy breakfast should contain milk or dairy products, cereal or bread, and fruit or fruit juice for their vitamins.

Each vitamin has an important role to play. Apart from vitamin D, your body is not able to produce vitamins for itself. You have to eat different foods to obtain them. Vitamin A is important for growth and resistance to infection, and for healthy skin and eyes. There are more than 12 kinds of vitamin B. They help the nerves, muscles, and digestive system to work properly. They are also useful in producing red blood cells and absorbing sugar.

Vitamin C helps you fight disease and keeps tissues and cells healthy. It can be easily destroyed by cooking.

Without vitamin D, your bones would be soft and your teeth brittle. It helps your body make use of calcium and phosphorus to keep your skeleton strong.

Vitamin E keeps skin and tissues healthy so that they'll keep working properly as you grow older.

Vitamin K plays a vital role in helping blood to clot.

Where can you find the vitamins that you need?

Vitamin A: in liver, egg yolk, butter, and milk

Vitamin B: in fresh meat, egg yolk, milk, meat, cereals, vegetables, and fruit

Vitamin C: in citrus fruits, kiwi fruit, potatoes, and vegetables

Vitamin D: in liver, egg yolk, butter, oily fish like mackerel, and cheese

Vitamin E: in milk, vegetable oil, wheat germ, and green vegetables

Vitamin K: in liver, eggs, meat, parsley, spinach, and cauliflower

The first thing you did when you were born was to take a great gulp of air. You gave a loud cry and started to breathe—and you have been breathing ever since. You can't stop breathing for more than a few moments—if you did, you'd turn blue and suffocate.

Oxygen in the air supports life on Earth. All of your cells need oxygen. The respiratory system is the body's way of supplying its cells with oxygen.

The respiratory system is like an upside-down tree with its branches in the lungs. The windpipe is the trunk; the bronchi are the main branches; the bronchioles, the smaller branches, end in a bunch of leaves—delicate air sacs called alveoli. You breathe air in through your nose and mouth. Tiny hairs inside your nose keep dirt and germs from going through the airways.

On a cold day you can see your breath because it is warmer than the air around you. Your warm breath forms a cloud of water vapor.

Down in your lungs, the air meets your blood in the alveoli. The blood takes oxygen from the air and gets rid of a waste gas called carbon dioxide, which leaves your body as you breathe out again.

How do you speak? Your vocal cords are stretched across the back of your throat, making a "voice box." As you breathe out, the air makes the cords vibrate and produce a sound, just as the cords of a harp vibrate when you touch them.

Your lungs have no muscles of their own. Instead, the diaphragm, a big muscle at the base of your lungs, pulls down. Your chest expands and air is sucked into the lungs. The diaphragm relaxes and arches up as you breathe out. You breathe in two times, in, out, in, out. You normally breathe without thinking about it, but you can make yourself take deeper, faster breaths.

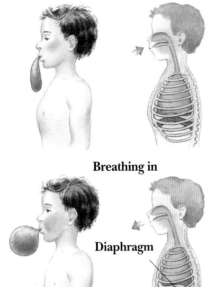

Breathing in

Diaphragm

Breathing out

What are hiccups? Hiccups are short, sharp, sudden breaths of air. The diaphragm contracts in jerks, making you gasp.

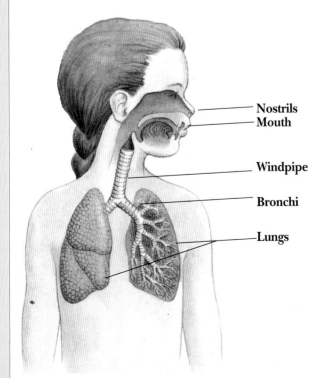

Nostrils
Mouth

Windpipe

Bronchi

Lungs

Colds, sinusitis, bronchitis, pneumonia

Sometimes it's difficult to breathe and swallow. Your nose is stuffed up and runs all the time; your voice is hoarse, and you're coughing. These are all infections in different parts of the respiratory system. Usually they get better on their own, or with the help of medicine. But if you have pneumonia or another serious illness, you have to go to the hospital.

When you cough and sneeze, you get rid of germs.

Allergies can be painful and irritating. At certain times of the year, especially in the spring and fall, some people can't stop sneezing and their eyes become red and streaming. These people suffer from hay fever—but in fact, they are allergic to the pollen produced by certain plants. Allergies to dust, feathers, fur, and cigarette smoke all set off the same symptoms.

Health warning

Smoking cigarettes can damage your lungs and lead to serious illnesses. Don't even give it a try!

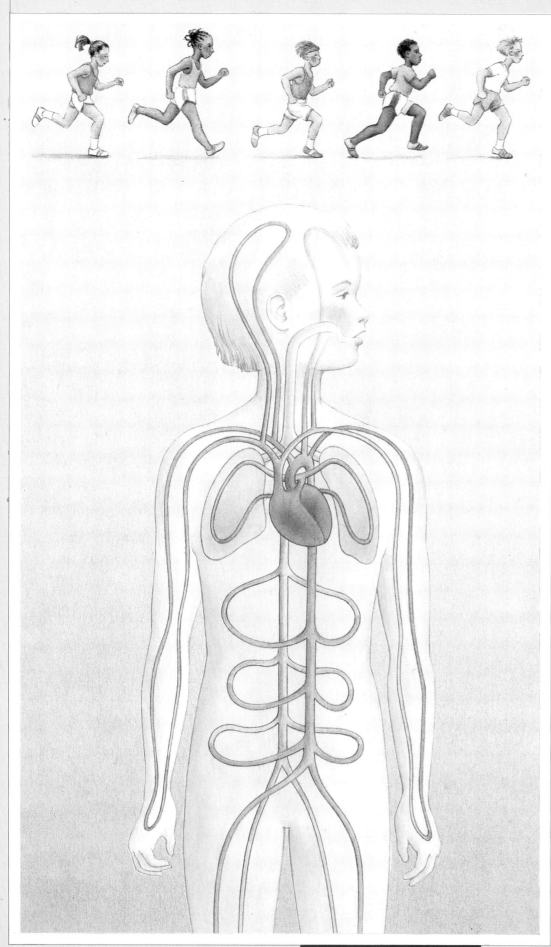

Your heart is the engine of your body. When your heart stops, your life has ended. That's why your heart is so precious. It's a hollow muscle about the size of your fist.

Your heart beats non-stop in your chest. It pumps, then rests—about 70 times a minute. As it works, the heart drives the circulatory system.

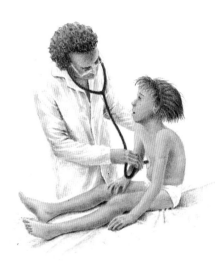

A doctor listens to your heartbeat through a stethoscope.

You can feel your heart beat faster when you have a big surprise or are excited or frightened. The rhythm speeds up when you are active and slows down when you are asleep.

The cardiovascular system: the arteries are shown in red, the veins in blue.

Thousands of miles of blood vessels

When you take your pulse, you can feel the throb of your heartbeat.

The heart has four chambers: two small ones at the top, called atria (just one is an atrium), and two larger ones at the bottom, called ventricles.

The heart is divided into two separate parts. The left side pumps red, oxygen-filled blood through your body. The right side takes in "used" blood, carrying the waste gas carbon dioxide, and sends it to your lungs. Fresh blood and the "used" blood never get mixed up.

Your heart pumps blood through your body's cardiovascular system. Blood travels in the blood vessels, tubes that can bend and grow smaller the farther they are from the heart, until they are microscopic.

The two types of blood vessels are arteries and veins. Arteries, shown in red, carry oxygen-filled blood from the heart to all the cells in your body.

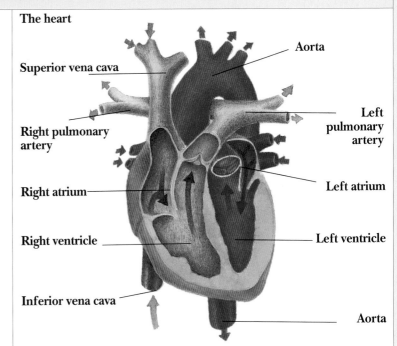

The heart

Superior vena cava

Right pulmonary artery

Right atrium

Right ventricle

Inferior vena cava

Aorta

Left pulmonary artery

Left atrium

Left ventricle

Aorta

Veins, shown in blue, carry used blood back to the heart and on to the lungs, where they will get rid of carbon dioxide gas. The blood system is like a one-way traffic system—blood goes around in only one direction; valves keep it from doubling back.

The coronary arteries, two small arteries, feed the heart. They measure only a small fraction of an inch in diameter. These tiny vessels can sometimes get blocked, often as a result of too much tobacco or cholesterol.

When the heart can't continue to pump, the person has a cardiac arrest, or heart attack. You can help to avoid heart disease by not smoking and not eating too many fatty foods.

Red blood cells carry oxygen around your body.

When you cut yourself, blood trickles out. You have about three quarts (2.8 l) of blood in your body; an adult has about five quarts (4.7 l). Blood is red and slightly sticky. It is made up of a clear liquid called plasma, in which thousands of tiny cells move. Some are red blood cells, some are white blood cells, and some are platelets.

A drop of blood on a microscope slide

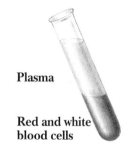

Plasma

Red and white blood cells

About 16 trillion red cells are in your blood. No wonder you can only see them under a microscope—they're so small.

Each cell has a job to do. Bone marrow in the center of your bones produces blood cells. Each blood cell lives for only three months, so your marrow works nonstop to make new ones.

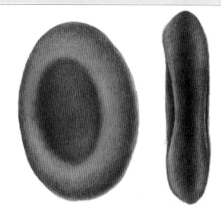

Cross section of a red blood cell (magnified 8,000 times). Red blood cells get their color from a substance called hemoglobin, which carries oxygen through the body.

Red blood cells form a transport system. They carry oxygen from the lungs to all the body's cells. Every organ is made up of millions and millions of cells. The red blood cells then carry carbon dioxide back to the lungs, which exhale it.

White blood cells fight infections. If you become ill, they multiply rapidly, move in, and attack the germs.

Adults who want to donate blood can visit specially equipped vans. Hospitals need stocks of blood for operations and emergencies.

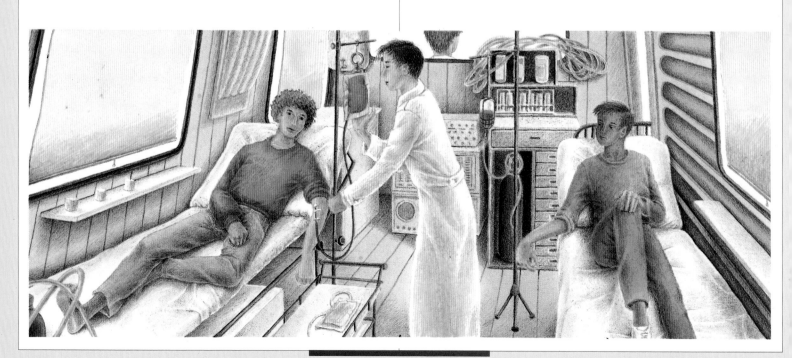

Blood is a complex liquid.

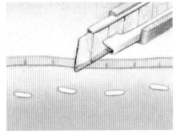
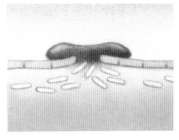

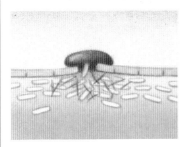
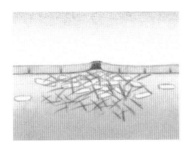

Platelets collect around a wound to form a clot.

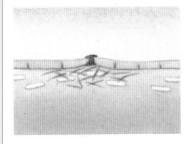
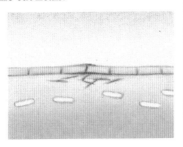

Underneath the clot, special cells repair the damage.
After a few days, the cut heals.

Platelets rush to block a break in a blood vessel. When you scrape your knee or cut yourself, platelets work to repair the wound. They bind with fibrin to form a clot, a sort of net to hold in the blood. As the clot dries, it turns into a scab. When the wound has healed, the scab falls off—its work is done and it leaves a small scar for awhile.

Don't scratch a scab off if you have a scrape. The scab keeps out germs.

Not everybody has the same type of blood. The four different blood groups are O, A, AB, and B. To find out the blood group to which you belong, you have a blood test. The lab tests your blood and gives you a card showing your blood group.

Knowing your blood type is important because not all the blood groups can be mixed. People with blood group O are called "universal donors." They can give their blood to anyone, but can only receive from group O. Group AB can only give blood to others of group AB, but they can receive blood from all the groups—they are universal receivers. Group A can give to A and to AB and receive from A and O. Group B can give to B and to AB, and receive from B and from O. There are also other substances in blood that complicate the matching process.

Sometimes you may get a nose bleed. It happens when a small vessel inside your nose tears. It looks as if the blood is pouring out, but a nosebleed is not usually serious.

The lymphatic system helps to fight disease. Lymph is a colorless liquid that travels around the body in lymph vessels carrying white blood cells. Across the path of the lymph vessels are small balls called lymph nodes, which swell up if you have an infection. Lymph nodes create a barrier against germs.

Two kidneys: the body's perfect filter system

Blood collects waste products from the cells of all the organs in your body. If all this waste were allowed to pile up, it would act like a poison. Your body has to get rid of it—which is the work of your two kidneys. Each is the shape of a kidney bean and a little smaller than your fist.

In the kidneys, blood goes through tiny vessels in contact with millions of tiny filtering units, and the waste products are filtered out just as they would be through a strainer. The waste matter, urea, mixes with water and forms urine; the freshly cleaned blood flows back to the heart. It's important to drink plenty of water to help the kidneys wash away waste.

Where does the urine go?

It collects in the bladder, which is like a little bag. When the bladder is full, nerves send messages to the brain that it's time to empty it. That's when you feel the need to urinate. If you wait too long, there may be an overflow.

Kidneys

Bladder

Urinary system seen from the front

What's the most obvious difference between a boy and a girl?

The lungs, heart, blood vessels, and digestive system all work in exactly the same way in both girls and boys.

This isn't true when it comes to the genitals—the equipment needed for human reproduction.

Little girls have all they will need to become mothers: two ovaries to make the ova, a uterus, and a vagina. Little boys have a penis and two testicles that will hold sperm. During puberty these reproductive organs become developed enough to do their jobs.

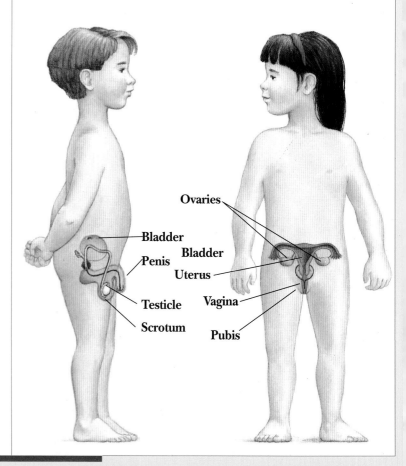

Ovaries

Bladder

Penis

Bladder

Uterus

Testicle

Vagina

Scrotum

Pubis

Puberty is a time of change. Boys and girls who have not reached the age of puberty can't make babies; their reproductive organs are not yet ready. Before the ovaries can make the ova, or the testicles the sperm, the body must go through a great change. It happens slowly over several years, but you can recognize it in all the physical and mental changes between the ages of nine and 16. Certain signs begin to appear—with boys, their voices get deeper and they start to grow body hair. With girls, their breasts grow and menstruation begins. Teenagers may put on weight and develop acne for awhile.

Your skeleton has 208 bones that hold you upright.

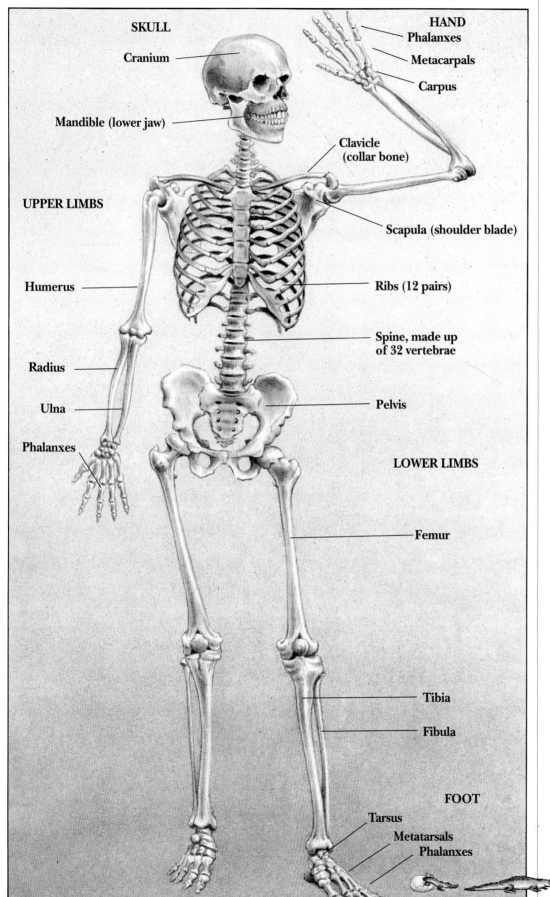

SKULL

Cranium

Mandible (lower jaw)

UPPER LIMBS

Humerus

Radius

Ulna

Phalanxes

HAND
Phalanxes
Metacarpals
Carpus

Clavicle
(collar bone)

Scapula (shoulder blade)

Ribs (12 pairs)

Spine, made up
of 32 vertebrae

Pelvis

LOWER LIMBS

Femur

Tibia

Fibula

FOOT
Tarsus
Metatarsals
Phalanxes

If you squeeze one of your fingers tightly, you will feel a hard bone. Without a skeleton, you wouldn't be able to stand up and move around.

Two hundred bones of all shapes and sizes are in your body. Some bones, such as ossicles, scaphoid, and coccyx, have very funny names.

Your smallest bones are inside your ear; the longest bone is the femur, your thigh bone. Others, like your teeth, don't look like bones at all. Some bones form the framework of your body, supporting it and holding it together. Others shield delicate organs—your brain is protected by a solid skull; your heart and lungs are safe behind the buffer of your ribcage.

It's a framework that is very much alive!

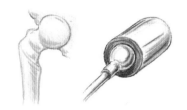 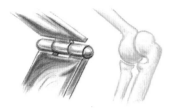

Not all joints work in the same way. A hip joint is a ball and socket joint—the head of one bone fits into the hollow of another.

A hinge joint works like the hinge on a door. The elbow and the knee are hinge joints.

Well-oiled hinges let you bend and twist.
Bands of tissue called ligaments hold together bones at the joints. The bone heads are cushioned with cartilage; an oily liquid called synovial fluid keeps the joints moving easily.

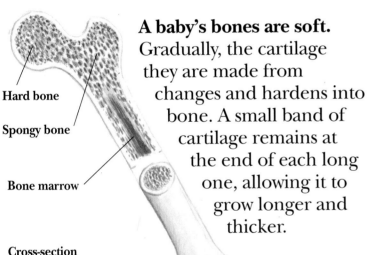

Hard bone

Spongy bone

Bone marrow

Cross-section of a femur

A baby's bones are soft.
Gradually, the cartilage they are made from changes and hardens into bone. A small band of cartilage remains at the end of each long one, allowing it to grow longer and thicker.

By the time you are an adult, the bands of growth cartilage at the end of each bone have turned into hard bone. Down the center of the bone runs the marrow, a jelly-like substance where blood cells are made.

Some animals continue to grow throughout their whole lives.

 **A broken bone can be mended.** Your bones are very strong, but they can still break if you have a bad fall. That break is called a fracture. A doctor X-rays the bone to see how badly it is broken.

Sometimes the bones have to be set, or put back in place, to help them mend properly. Then the doctor puts a cast on the broken limb to hold it steady and give the bone a chance to heal. Healing can take several weeks.

Your bones continue producing new cells—otherwise they could never mend once they had been broken.

A callus forms where the bone was broken.

When the cast comes off, exercises help to strengthen the limb that has been hurt.

Your skeleton's bones are made of calcium and phosphorus.
That is why it is important to eat plenty of fish and dairy products. These types of foods help your bones grow and be strong.

Your bones and muscles make a reliable team. It would be impossible to have one without the other. Without muscles, your bones wouldn't be able to move. Tendons attach muscles to your bones. Tendons make the bones move by contracting and relaxing; one muscle shortens, the other stretches out.

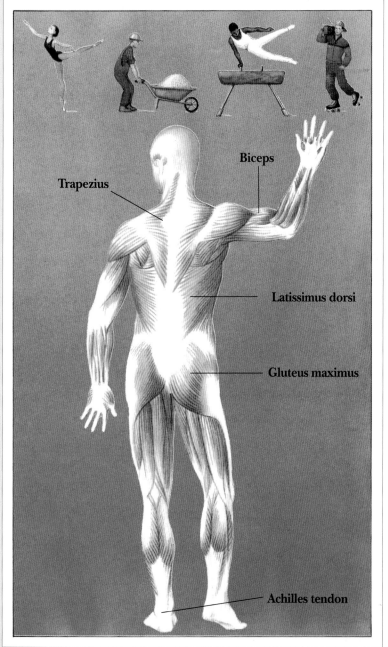

Trapezius

Biceps

Latissimus dorsi

Gluteus maximus

Achilles tendon

Nerves control the muscles. When your brain gives the order to a muscle to contract, nerves carry a message and the appropriate muscle obeys. Muscles cannot push; they can only pull. That's why they often come in pairs and work together to provide a range of movement.

Your body has more than 600 muscles. Some are large, like the ones in your calves or thighs. Others are small, like your tongue or the ones that make your eyes move.

Muscles aren't all made the same way or in the same shape. Skeletal, or striped, muscles are the ones you decide to move. Some, such as your biceps, are shaped like a spindle. Others, such as your back muscles, are shaped like a fan; and still others, such as your lips and eyelids, are like links.

All the muscles that make up the walls of your stomach and intestines are smooth muscle. They work automatically; you can't control what these muscles do even if you think about them.

Your heart is a special muscle. Like all the others, nerves control the cardiac, or heart, muscle—but the heart also has an automatic mechanism sort of like a battery, which means it can beat on its own.

Some baby animals can get up and gallop away the moment they are born. Humans can't do that—probably because we don't need to; a lion isn't waiting around the corner to eat us!

Your muscles enable you to hold and control things. A baby finds it difficult to pick up a thread between two fingers.

The right foods provide energy to play a sport. Drink plenty of water afterward.

Sometimes your muscles hurt. Do you ever feel stiff after you have overworked muscles that aren't used to exercise? Or have you ever had a cramp, in your calf perhaps? Waste products have built up and caused a sharp pain, a warning to rest for a while. If, by accident, you pull a ligament in your ankle or your knee, you will have a sprain.

Take care of your muscles. Athletes always warm up before playing or performing. It's a good way to prepare your muscles for the effort you are about to ask of them. They will work better, and you will have less chance of injury.

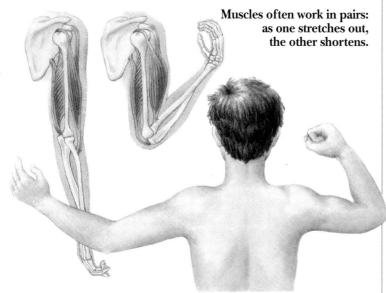

Muscles often work in pairs: as one stretches out, the other shortens.

Newborn human babies can't even hold up their head. Gradually, as their bones harden, their muscles grow stronger too, and they learn to make different movements.

Muscles need energy if they are to work properly. Energy comes from the food you eat. As it is digested, the food is broken down into tiny particles that the blood carries to give energy to all the cells in your muscles.

From your head to your toes, your body is wrapped in skin.

This feels soft; that feels cold—ouch, that hurts! Your skin has nerve endings that relay what is happening outside your body. But your skin can show what's going on inside your body too. You blush with embarrassment; you get pale with fright. Spots are a sign of illness or an allergy.

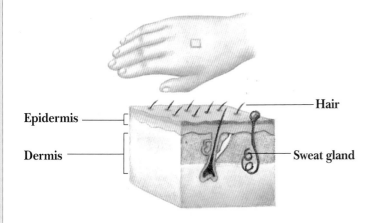

Epidermis

Dermis

Hair

Sweat gland

Your skin is made up of two layers. The epidermis is the thin top layer, with the thicker dermis underneath. The tiny holes in it are called pores.

Everyone's skin is slightly different. The pigment that gives your skin color is called melanin. Your skin will be darker or lighter, depending on the dispersal of melanin in it.

Your skin contains a lot of water. If your body wasn't wrapped in an envelope of skin, the water would run out or evaporate in the air. Then your body would look like a shriveled-up prune!

Your skin does not just keep water in; it also keeps it out. It produces a sort of grease called sebum, which makes you waterproof. If you weren't waterproof, you would swell up like a sponge in the bathtub.

You can help your skin do its work by wearing light clothes in warm weather and dressing warmly in cold weather.

Your skin helps you adapt to hot and cold. When it's hot, small glands produce sweat, which cools you down as it evaporates. Your blood vessels open up and rise to the surface of your skin to help cool the blood. That's why you look flushed.

When it's cold, your blood vessels contract to keep in heat, and the hairs on your arms and legs stand up—you have goose bumps.

Skin protects you from germs. Healthy skin makes a strong barrier against bacteria.

It's important to look after your skin.

Your face is never covered up, so it needs a good wash twice a day.

How do you wash? Many people take a bath or a shower every day because dirt and dust stick to sebum. As you wash yourself, you remove the old layer of grease. It's replaced at once with a new one.

Bumps and bruises

Your skin is strong; it's good protection. But accidents happen now and then. It is important to clean cuts and scrapes. If you have a bump, the blood and lymph vessels can be crushed slightly, even if the skin is not broken. Liquid spills out and causes a swollen bump. Special cells in the surrounding tissues help repair the damage. In a few days, the swelling disappears.

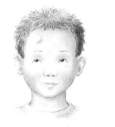

You fall over, and there you are with a bump, scrape, or bruise—and if you're unlucky, all three at once!

The same sort of thing happens when you're bruised. The small blood vessels get crushed, and a pool of blood forms under the skin. Blood vessels mend quickly, and blood soon stops leaking out. Before they disappear, bruises change color from dark purple to blue, then yellow.

Be especially careful of burns and scalds!

Boiling water, a hot iron, electricity, a light bulb that's switched on . . . many things around your home can burn you. Skin can't stand very high temperatures.

When you burn yourself, you lose a protective layer of skin, and you're in danger of losing your body's fluids. All burns are painful.

A first-degree burn makes your skin turn red; a second-degree burn causes blisters; a third-degree burn starts to destroy the skin, turning it black.

Sun burns too. You need to be careful not to get sunburned, especially if you have fair skin. Normally, your skin protects itself from the sun by producing more melanin. Skin becomes darker to better resist the sun's rays. A protective cream or lotion, sunscreen, gives your skin an extra barrier against damaging rays from the sun. Scientists now know that too much exposure to sun can cause skin cancer. So when you're outside in the sun, be wise! Remember sunscreen, sunglasses, and a hat.

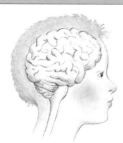

What controls and organizes all the different body systems? What enables you to have feelings, thoughts, and ideas? The nervous system, highly perfected and complex, is made up of the brain, the spinal cord, and 43 pairs of nerves. The brain itself is made up of the cerebrum, the cerebellum, and the brain stem.

Your brain is made up of billions of nerve cells, called neurons. Cells like these are also found in the spinal cord and the nerves. Neurons, shaped like tiny stars, have elongated arms trailing in all directions to pick up messages from other cells.

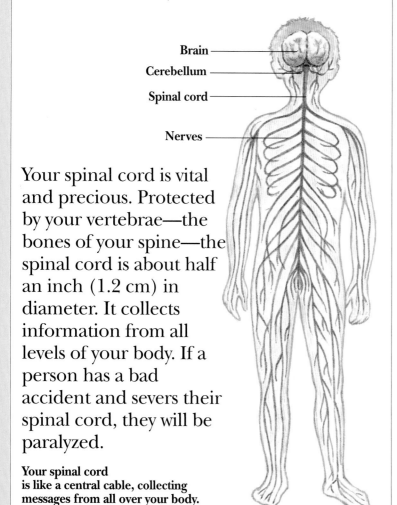

Brain
Cerebellum
Spinal cord
Nerves

Your spinal cord is vital and precious. Protected by your vertebrae—the bones of your spine—the spinal cord is about half an inch (1.2 cm) in diameter. It collects information from all levels of your body. If a person has a bad accident and severs their spinal cord, they will be paralyzed.

Your spinal cord is like a central cable, collecting messages from all over your body.

A baby is born with all its neurons in place. While still in their mother's womb, babies acquire millions of new neurons every minute, so they have hundreds of billions in reserve. This is a good thing, because neurons do not renew themselves, and you start to lose them from the age of 20 onward. If a nerve cell is destroyed, it cannot be replaced.

Human brains have evolved into an extraordinary, ultra-perfected organ. Human beings are the only creatures to have such a high-performance brain.

Cradled inside your skull, the cerebrum is divided into two hemispheres: left and right. Each is wrapped in a sort of gray matter called the cerebral cortex.

When you are young, the cortex is smooth. As you grow older, it creases, and the surface begins to look like a walnut.

Make your hands into fists, put them one against the other, and you'll have an idea of the size and shape of your brain.

Has anyone ever called you a birdbrain when you've done something silly? That's because animals have brains that are far less developed than humans' brains.

Think of your brain as the center of a telephone system. The nerves are the network of telephone lines relaying messages. Sensory nerves carry information from your skin and sensory organs to your brain; motor nerves carry messages from the brain to your muscles.

Thousands of messages, or nerve impulses, circulate throughout your body all the time. The brain receives these messages through the neurons in your nerves and spinal cord. It uses neurons to send out instructions too.

Some of these messages are under your control. The walk light turns on, and you know you can cross the road. The phone rings, and you pick up the receiver. You can direct your body to do all kinds of things.

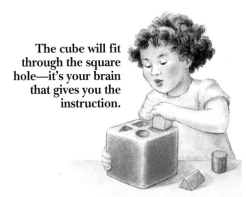

The cube will fit through the square hole—it's your brain that gives you the instruction.

Many messages are independent of your will. One area of your brain looks after the rhythm of your heartbeat, your breathing, and your digestion. This area makes sure you sleep, that your glands work, and that you eat—all of those things that happen all the time, without you even thinking about them. If something frightens you, your heart begins to beat rapidly, and your breath comes in gasps, whether you like it or not.

The brain regulates the five senses of smell, taste, touch, sight, and hearing.

You can make your brain perform better, especially your memory, if you exercise it. Scientists now know that the cortex is divided into different zones, each specializing in a different set of responses and actions.

The different zones in the brain:
1. Motor area controlling movement
2. Sensory area
3. Sight
4. Hearing
5. Smell
6. Speech

Each hemisphere receives messages from the opposite side of the body and also directs the activities of the opposite side. Your right hand touches something hot: the message arrives in the left hemisphere of your brain, which sends the instruction to take your hand away.

You learn about the world through your senses. You can see beautiful landscapes, hear music, taste delicious food, smell the scent of flowers, and feel the softness of their petals.

What are the five senses? Sight, hearing, smell, taste, and touch. Your eyes, ears, nose, tongue, and skin are your sensory organs.

Each one detects sensations and sends messages to your brain through the sensory nerves. Each sense has a corresponding zone in the cerebral cortex. Your brain then sends out instructions to your muscles through the motor nerves.

Using and developing your senses

If you do not pay attention to your senses, you may find yourself living a dull, muffled life. But if you concentrate on what the senses tell you, you will find that they open up a world of variety—your senses will help you get the best out of life.

If you have lost or were born without one of your senses, you've probably developed the others far more than your friends who have all five. A person who is blind often has keen senses of touch and hearing.

Animals have highly developed senses. Often, one sense will be stronger than all the rest. Birds have little sense of smell, but they are sharp-sighted. Fish have a strong sense of smell, and they also have special auditory organs on their skin that work like ears. Snails use their antennae to taste. A snake collects smells with its forked tongue, which flickers in and out, picking up scents from the air.

Each animal uses sight, touch, hearing, taste, and smell in its own particular way.

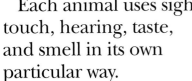

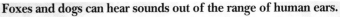

Foxes and dogs can hear sounds out of the range of human ears.

Some animals seem to have a special sense. Something terrible is going to happen. What can it be? The hens are panicking, the horses trembling, and the swallows twittering—long before humans have any idea that something is wrong. Animals are particularly sensitive to vibrations, so they can judge where there is going to be an earthquake, for example.

Before flies take wing, they stretch out their antennae to find out how hard the wind is blowing.

A cicada hears through organs on either side of its abdomen.

A cricket's ears are on its legs.

Female mosquitoes, which feed on blood, use their antennae to sense the presence of a warm-blooded animal or person from several yards away.

Dolphins and whales, like all cetaceans, have a sixth sense—sonar. They send out sounds that bounce off the objects around them. The nature and direction of the echo tell them the shape of the object and how far away it is.

The eye is a delicate organ.

What is an eye? The eye is a soft globe protected by eyelids. It is set in a cavity called the orbit. Your eyes move a lot in all directions—even if you think they are still. Muscles in the orbit hold the eyes in place. Tears wash the eye constantly, keeping it clean and moist. The eyelids spread the tears across the eyeball and blink about once every 10 seconds.

A horse cannot see clearly things that are directly ahead, but it can see a long way to either side.

Humans cannot see as far to the side as a horse can, but we do see more clearly, because the vision of each eye overlaps.

Eagles are sharp-sighted and can spot their prey, a mouse for example, from a great height.

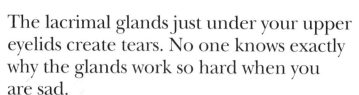
Eyelids and eyelashes protect the eyes.

1. Cornea   2. Iris
3. Pupil   4. Lens
5. Retina   6. Optic nerve

The lacrimal glands just under your upper eyelids create tears. No one knows exactly why the glands work so hard when you are sad.

A transparent membrane called the cornea protects the iris, which can be brown, blue, gray, or green. The black dot in the center of the iris is in fact an opening, called the pupil. The lens behind the pupil changes shape according to whether the eye is looking at things close up or far away; this is called focusing. Light passes through the pupil and the lens and falls on the retina at the back of the eye.

To see things in three dimensions, both eyes need to be working properly. The optic nerve carries information from the retina to the brain. Your left eye can see a little more to the left, and the right eye can see a little more to the right. As the lens focuses an image on the retina, it runs the picture upside down. When the brain receives the information, it turns the image the right way up again.

Eye doctors are called ophthalmologists. They use a special instrument to see through the pupil to the retina, right at the back of the eye.

Muscles that fix the eyes to the orbit allow them to move quickly and in every direction.

Dragonflies have up to 40,000 tiny lenses in each eye. Their eyes cover almost all of their heads.

Do you wear glasses? If you do, it is because your eyes do not work perfectly. If your eyeball is too long, you are nearsighted. You can see things that are near quite clearly, but things that are a long way off look blurred. If your eyeball is too short, you are farsighted, and the opposite is true. Glasses help to focus the image on the retina.

If you are astigmatic, it means that your lens or cornea is an irregular shape, and you will have blurred or double vision. In fact, no one's eyes are perfectly round. Older people tend to need glasses because their lenses and muscles aren't as supple as they used to be and don't work as well. Older people are usually farsighted.

If a person squints or looks cross-eyed, it means that one of the eye muscles isn't directing the eye correctly. Doing eye exercises often can solve the problem, but sometimes an operation is necessary.

Glasses are made for just one pair of eyes. Your friend's glasses won't be much help to you.

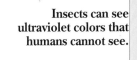

Insects can see ultraviolet colors that humans cannot see.

The ophthalmologist has your glasses made especially for you. When you are older, you may prefer to wear contact lenses, which are small round lenses that you learn to put directly onto the surface of the eye.

When it is dark, the pupil opens wide to let in as much light as possible. In bright light, it shrinks.

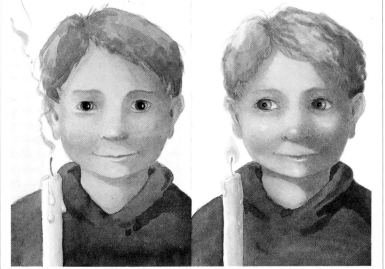

A nearsighted person sees distant things with a blurred outline. Glasses make the image clear.

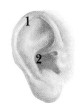

You can rest your eyes, but your ears work all the time. They never stop picking up noises. Even before you were born, you heard your mother's voice. Later you learned to recognize different words and then say them. From birth, your hearing worked as an alarm system, warning you of dangers before you could see them.

Outer ear
1. Auricle 2. Auditory canal

Middle ear
3. Tympanum (eardrum) 4. Ossicles (bones)

Inner ear
5. Semicircular canals
6. Cochlea

The tympanum is a fine sheet that vibrates like a drum skin. The louder the sound entering the ear, the more the tympanum (the eardrum) vibrates. Behind it lie three tiny bones called the stirrup, the hammer, and the anvil (they're each named after their shape). These bones transmit vibrations to the cochlea, a snail-shaped tube full of liquid. It turns the vibrations into nerve impulses, which are sent along the auditory nerve to the brain. The brain tells you where they come from and what they mean.

If you throw a pebble into the water, ripples move outward from where it fell. In the same way, sound waves move through the air.

Try this. Stretch a rubber band between your finger and thumb. If you twang it, you will see it vibrate and hear a sound. Sounds are vibrations that move through the air.

You can't hear every sound. Ultrasounds are too high-pitched for humans to hear, but a dog, with its sharp ears, responds to an ultrasonic whistle.

The semicircular canals in your inner ear give you a sense of balance. If you spin around a few times and then stop, you will find it hard to keep your balance. This is because the liquid in your ears is still moving, even though you are not. The same thing happens when you feel seasick on board a boat.

Crooked noses, long noses, squashed-up noses, turned-up noses . . . noses come in all shapes and sizes, and the way they smell varies too. You could say a person's sense of smell is like his or her fingerprint: it is unique. No two people have the same identical sense of smell.

A smell is made of countless tiny chemical particles that float in the air that you breathe. Inside your nose are smell detectors, called olfactory receptors, covered with tiny hairs. Several thousand different smells bombard these receptors.

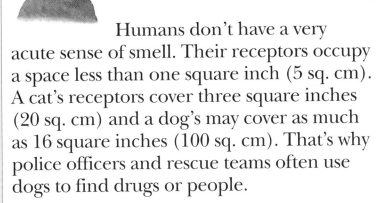

Humans don't have a very acute sense of smell. Their receptors occupy a space less than one square inch (5 sq. cm). A cat's receptors cover three square inches (20 sq. cm) and a dog's may cover as much as 16 square inches (100 sq. cm). That's why police officers and rescue teams often use dogs to find drugs or people.

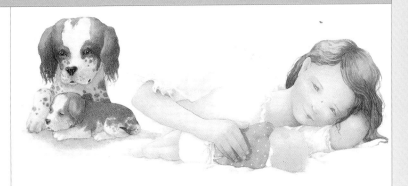

The receptors report the different smells to your brain, and your brain decides what they mean. A delicious smell of freshly baked bread wafting from the kitchen will make you feel hungry.

The sense of smell is there from the beginning. A newborn baby recognizes her mother's smell, and a mother can recognize the scent of her own baby. This bond is very important. It comforts the baby and becomes the first means of communication she has with the world.

The scent linking mothers and babies is even more important among animals. Smell is often like an identity card. An ant colony will reject a strange ant passing by because it does not smell right to them.

People who invent perfumes have a particularly well developed sense of smell. They can detect the subtlest differences between scents and are able to pick out nearly 4,000 different ones.

How do you taste things? You use your tongue.

A child's taste buds are much more sensitive than an adult's.

Taste buds cover your tongue. They look like tiny spots, and you have nearly 2,000 of them. Eating without them would be boring. Most foods would taste the same. Each taste bud is sensitive to a particular kind of taste.

Your tongue is better at telling the difference between sweet and salty tastes than between bitter and sour ones. Even before a baby is born, he prefers sweet-tasting things. Fortunately, a growing child learns to enjoy other tastes as well.

The tongue is sensitive to temperature and consistency as well as to taste.

●Bitter ● Salt
●Sour ● Sweet

Keep your taste buds exercised—try out different foods. Your sense of taste will improve as you learn to appreciate subtle differences in foods. You may even become a *gourmet*. That's a French word for someone who is an expert on food and wine.

The four basic tastes are sweet (sugar), sour (lemon), bitter (coffee), and salty (salt).

The sense of taste is closely linked to the sense of smell. If you have a cold, it is difficult to tell what things taste like. The best way to take a horrible-tasting medicine is to hold your nose as you swallow it. This is because much of what you think is taste is really smell.

You may be left with a nasty taste in your mouth, but if the medicine is going to make you better, it's worth it.

Every country has different traditions about what tastes good—some people like spicy foods, others prefer sweet ones.

French people like eating snails, but some people in other countries can't bear the thought of eating them. How would you feel if you visited the Amazon and the people there offered you a dish of grilled caterpillars? Would you eat roasted snake in Indonesia?

The sense of touch is located in the skin.

Your skin collects messages from the world around you. It is sensitive to a gentle touch, the soft warmth of a sweater, the cold of an ice cube, or the prick of an injection.

Your skin reacts when it is touched. Your skin is full of sensitive nerve endings. These send instant messages to the zones of the brain that specialize in feeling. These zones tell you how to react. For example, if someone steps on your toe, it hurts and your brain tells you to get your foot out of the way! Although it feels unpleasant, pain is helpful—it's like an emergency siren warning us when something is wrong.

The scaly skin of a chicken's foot and the tough hooves of a deer or a horse are not as sensitive as the skin of a snake.

Babies explore the world around them by putting things in their mouths. That is where the skin is most sensitive, and where they can learn a great deal. An injection is usually given into an arm or buttocks, where the skin is less sensitive.

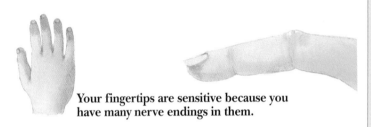

Your fingertips are sensitive because you have many nerve endings in them.

Animals have different ways of using their sense of touch. Spiders constantly spin and repair their webs, using the hairs on their feet as their organs of touch. Bees can tell the shape of things accurately by using their antennae. The tiny shrew uses its whiskers to find its way around.

Some of the different sensations you feel when you touch:

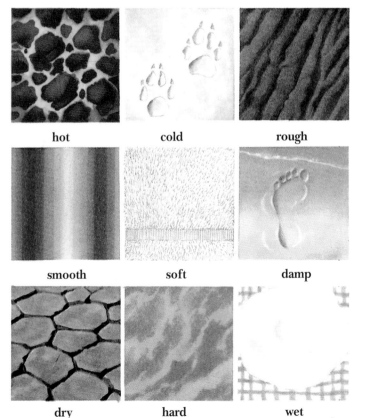

hot   cold   rough

smooth   soft   damp

dry   hard   wet

Blindfold yourself and try to recognize different fruits by the way they feel and smell.

At the end of every day . . .

When the sun sinks down below the horizon and the last pink rays fade from the trees and rooftops, you know that it will soon be dark and time for you to go to bed. The birds begin to roost, cows in the field head for the barn, flowers close their petals, and the family dog curls up in its favorite spot. But it's now that other creatures start to wake up. Owls, bats, and badgers hunt at night and sleep during the day. They are nocturnal.

You spend about one-third of your life asleep. When you were a newborn baby, you slept nearly all the time, day and night. Now, your life follows the pattern of the sun more closely—awake during the hours of daylight and asleep at night.

Early birds and night owls
Are you more awake in the morning or in the evening? People's body rhythms vary, and so does the amount of sleep each person wants and needs.

Children need a lot of sleep—at least 10 or 11 hours each night.

How do you know when you're getting sleepy? Your brain has been working hard all day. Now it sends signals that it's time to rest.

Your muscles relax; you start to yawn. You can't think straight and your eyelids feel heavy. Your eyes start to feel itchy, and adults say, "It's time for bed!" When you settle down to sleep, get comfortable. Lie in your favorite position in bed; everyone has one that works the best. Do you have a favorite toy that you like to cuddle?

Is it sometimes hard to get to sleep? Drinking warm milk may help you get to sleep. A bath before bedtime will warm you up and help you relax.

Before you set off on the mysterious journey into sleep, ask someone to read you a story. It will help you feel happy and content.

It's important to feel safe. If you don't like the dark, leave the bedroom door ajar, or turn on a night-light. Once your body is at ease, relax your mind and think of nice things. Good night, sleep well!

By measuring brain waves—the electric signals given out by your brain—scientists have begun to understand more about sleep.

It is made up of cycles; each lasts about two hours. You may go through four or five cycles in a night. Each sleep cycle has several different stages.

Insomnia is when you can't sleep.

At first you sleep lightly, then more deeply until you are "sleeping like a log." Then, under your closed eyelids, your eyes start to move rapidly. You are deeply asleep, but the neurons in your brain are as active as when you were awake. You are dreaming.

In a period of deep sleep, you may snore or talk in your sleep. Some people even sleepwalk.

Your brain is busy while you're asleep.

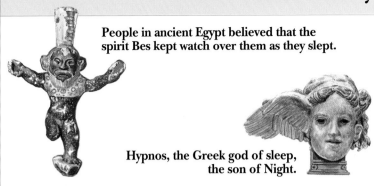

People in ancient Egypt believed that the spirit Bes kept watch over them as they slept.

Hypnos, the Greek god of sleep, the son of Night.

One cycle ends, and another begins. When you have had enough sleep, you wake up naturally at the end of a cycle. If your alarm clock goes off when you are in a deep sleep, it's a shock—it may take you a little while to remember where you are and what day it is.

Sleep is not a waste of time! Many things happen when you're asleep, not just vital rest. Dreams help your brain sort out what happened during the day. You grow, especially at the beginning of the night as growth hormones are released. There's an old expression that "sleep is a great healer." You often find that you wake up with the answer to a problem that was on your mind when you went to sleep. If you weren't allowed to sleep, you'd die. And if you weren't allowed to dream, you'd probably go crazy.

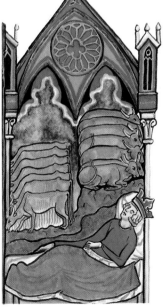

A Bible story describes the dream of an ancient Egyptian pharaoh. He dreamed that seven fat cows were eaten by seven thin ones. He was told that Egypt would have seven rich years, followed by seven years of drought and poverty. Apparently, the dream came true.

Not all dreams are pleasant ones.
Sometimes you may dream of frightening things. You wake up with a jump, your heart racing. You need to calm down before you can go back to sleep again.

The meaning of dreams
During the 19th century, Sigmund Freud researched the meaning of dreams (Freud studied the nervous system). He said that in people's dreams their unconscious thoughts —all the things in your mind you keep hidden even from yourself—come alive.

Germs are everywhere: in the air, in the ground, and in your body.

Have you ever heard anyone say, "I've got a bug"? This means that a germ has made them ill.

Germs are living things. There are millions of them, so tiny that you can only see them with a microscope. There are three types of germs. They are called bacteria, viruses, and fungi.

Bacteria are very small. They reproduce quickly by dividing into two. The two types of bacteria are bacilli, shaped like little sticks, and cocci, which are round or oval.

Viruses are some of the smallest known living things. They are not able to multiply on their own, so they live as parasites inside living cells, which they destroy as they grow. If a virus gets into your body, you get sick. The word virus means poison.

Fungi are microscopic. One is called a fungus; more than one are called fungi. They are often the cause of skin diseases.

Are germs ever useful? Some bacteria are harmless, and some are actually helpful. People have been making use of bacteria for hundreds of years without realizing it.

Staying warm in bed is a good way to help your body to get better.

Shivering, feeling sick, and getting a temperature are all signs that you have an infection.

Bacteria make bread dough rise, and wine, beer, and yogurt ferment. Inside your intestines, billions of bacteria help your digestion. They are called intestinal flora.

Unfortunately, other germs are your enemies. If they succeed in getting through your body's natural barriers—your skin, your tonsils, the hairs in your nose, and the acid in your stomach—you may start to feel sick. One of the easiest ways to keep germs out is to wash your hands often and well.

Medicines of the past

War breaks out between your body and the germ invaders! Your temperature rises as your body begins to attack germs. This is one of your body's defense mechanisms because heat kills germs.

The lymph nodes in the lymphatic system near the infection swell up and harden, joining in the battle against infection.

White blood cells are like soldiers, sent into action to defend the body against the invaders. Your bone marrow speeds up production to make extra reinforcements.

Some bacteria are friendly, others are harmful.

Bacteria cause some illnesses.
Typhoid, cholera, whooping cough, diphtheria, tuberculosis, tetanus, smallpox, leprosy, and scarlet fever all used to be dreaded killer diseases that spread from person to person. Now, due to vaccinations and antibiotics, they can be controlled, and, in most cases, cured.

Some plants can be used as medicines . . . or poisons!

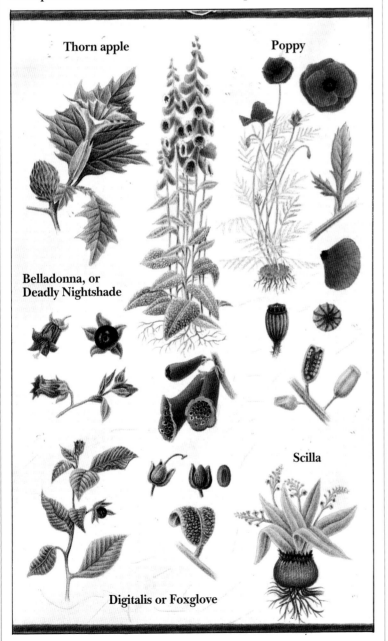

Thorn apple

Poppy

Belladonna, or Deadly Nightshade

Scilla

Digitalis or Foxglove

Viruses cause other illnesses. Viruses often cause coughs, colds, sore throats, and stomach upsets. They can also cause most of the childhood illnesses that are highly infectious and can spread through a classroom. Usually, you get them only once because your body makes antibodies to defend itself against the virus in the future. These antibodies stay with you for life, making you immune to the disease. Measles, chicken pox, German measles, and mumps are all caused by viruses and are rarely serious. Certain types of flu (influenza), yellow fever, hepatitis, and poliomyelisis are more dangerous. Many of the illnesses that viruses cause can be avoided with vaccinations.

People take medicines in many ways: as pills or syrups, as drops or ointment applied directly to the infected area, as suppositories to insert into the rectum, or by injection.

Cancer is not caused by germs. Abnormal cells in one part of the body can start to multiply and group together to form a lump, called a tumor. No one knows why they start to behave like this, and it is sometimes a difficult process to stop. If the tumor or lump is malignant (harmful), the cells from it may break away and damage other healthy cells, spreading the disease. Often it is possible to destroy the tumor, or reduce its size, and cure the cancer.

During the 19th century, a French scientist named Louis Pasteur discovered that it was possible to destroy harmful bacteria in milk if it was heated to a high temperature. This "pasteurized" milk would keep for several days.

The discovery of vaccine
Now that he knew how to weaken bacteria, he became interested in human illnesses. In 1885 he discovered that if he injected his patients with a dose of weakened bacteria, they did not seem to get worse; in fact, the germs seemed to strengthen the body's natural defenses. Pasteur had discovered the principle of vaccination. He saved his first patient, a boy who had been bitten by a rabid dog, from the deadly disease of rabies by treating him with a vaccine. The boy did not develop rabies.

Viruses are more difficult to kill than bacteria. No medicine nor antibiotic can kill a virus. It's not easy to get rid of them!

Luckily, the body often learns to defend itself on its own.

Important parts of your body's defense system are the antibodies the white blood cells make. Antibodies destroy harmful bacteria and viruses and neutralize the poisons they produce. Sometimes a particular germ may prove too strong, but if the antibodies win, they remain in the body to destroy that germ if it should ever reappear.

Vaccinations give you protection in advance. When you are vaccinated, you are injected with a weak dose of a certain virus. Your body starts to produce a stock of antibodies against it. If you come into contact with the same virus again, it will not make you ill. Babies are more at risk from illness before they have been vaccinated.

Making a vaccine

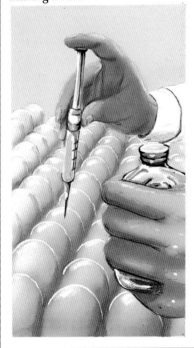

A research laboratory

The older you get, the more germs you meet, and the stronger your defenses grow.

New vaccines are discovered through research. Since Louis Pasteur, many more vaccines have been discovered to deal with tuberculosis, diphtheria, tetanus, and many other illnesses that bacteria cause—illnesses that used to be fatal. Now you can be vaccinated against all childhood illnesses, even chicken pox. Sometimes, even if you have been vaccinated against them, you can catch mumps or measles, but only in a mild form.

The trouble is, new viruses keep appearing. Doctors first recognized the AIDS virus in 1980. Scientists now know much about the virus, but no one has yet found a vaccine against it. AIDS is a serious illness that attacks the body's defense systems. A person who is suffering from AIDS has difficulty fighting off infections and eventually dies. There is hope, though, for people with AIDS. Doctors and scientists have found ways to help people with AIDS live longer, and they are working to find a cure.

To make a vaccine, the virus has to be grown, or "cultivated," on living animal matter. Here, fertilized eggs are being used in the manufacture of a flu vaccine.

If you are seriously ill, or you need an operation . . .

Ambulance

In hospitals, nurses and doctors work in shifts to give you care 24 hours a day. If there is an emergency, no time is wasted—all the needed equipment is brought in and doctors specializing in certain illnesses, or different parts of the body, can be at your side within minutes.

Samples of blood or urine, which may help in diagnosing an illness, are sent to the hospital laboratory immediately. Operating rooms are available in case of an emergency. X-rays, ultrasound, and other imaging equipment can show doctors pictures of the inside of the body.

Everything in an operating room is kept as clean as possible to avoid infection. Doctors and nurses wear hats, masks, gloves, and gowns and cover the patient with drapes.

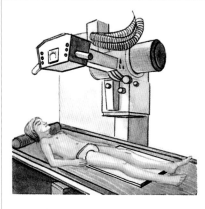
Radiography: an X-ray is being taken.

What if the surgeon decides to operate?
The doctors explain what's going to happen. Before surgery, the anesthetist gives you an injection so that you won't feel pain. The anesthetist may ask you to count backward from 10—you will probably be asleep before you reach eight. When you wake up, the operation will be over. You can hardly believe it—you think you're still waiting to go into the operating room!

Sometimes the anesthetist gives you gas to put you to sleep.

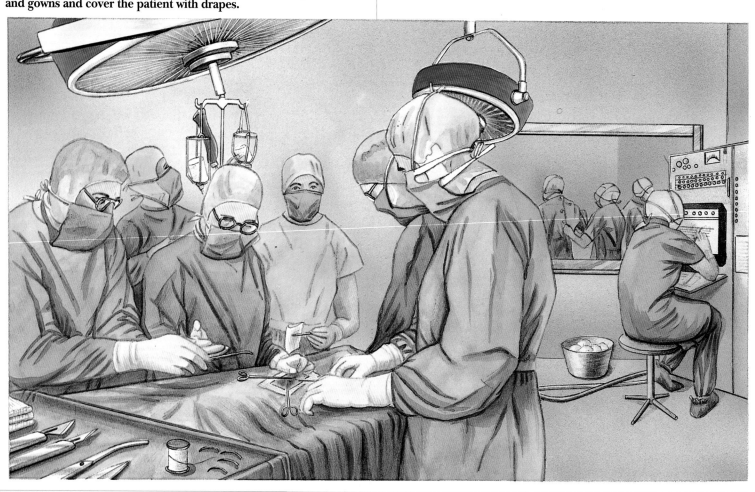

A day in the hospital

You usually get better quickly in the hospital. You stay in an area where all the other patients are children too: it's called a pediatric ward. It's comforting to see that you aren't the only one who is ill, and often you make very good friends.

The mornings are kept for medical tests and a visit from your doctor. You may be surprised to find that the hospital isn't a very restful place. The mornings are busy; there are beds to change and examinations to 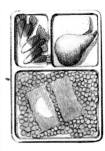 carry out. You may need an X-ray. If you are too ill to walk, nurses may use a wheelchair to take you to the X-ray department. In the morning, your doctor comes to check on you.

In the afternoon, your friends and family can come and visit you. Lunch is early in hospitals. There is always a choice and usually the food is good. Afterward, there's time to rest before your visitors arrive.

Then you can play in the game room, read, or watch television. Children who have to stay in the hospital for a long time have lessons as well—just when you thought you were on a vacation!

It's not always easy to get to sleep at night because hospitals can be noisy places. But it's reassuring to know there is always someone looking after you. Everyone in the hospital is working hard to help you get well.

Your doctor comes to see you on his or her rounds.

Young patients can play in the game room.

Teachers give lessons to children who have to stay in the hospital for a long time.

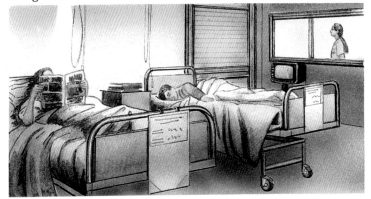
Nurses are on duty around the clock.

Your body is like a well-designed machine.

It's a clever machine that runs beautifully, but you must take care of it. From time to time, the machine breaks down—sometimes seriously—and you have to repair it. Scientists have made so much progress that modern medicine can now cure many things that go wrong. One of the best ways to stay well is to keep your body healthy. Eat well, exercise, keep yourself clean, and get enough sleep.

Practice a sport that you enjoy.
Physical exercise is vital for a healthy body.

At a health clinic, the staff checks your height, weight, sight, and hearing, and gives vaccinations.

Keeping clean is important to your health, and it helps you feel good about yourself.

It's good to challenge yourself, to learn new things, and to exercise your mind and body. Pick something you like doing, be realistic about your capabilities, and do it at your own speed. Sometimes, before you try, you may not feel like making an effort, but afterward you'll feel good about what you've accomplished.

A healthy mind in a healthy body

Everything can't always go according to plan, but that shouldn't keep you from having confidence in yourself. Everyone is different; each person is unique and special. Did you know that the people who live longest are those who keep alert and active? It's never too late to learn something new!

Personal hygiene is important. After you've been to the bathroom, always wash your hands to get rid of any germs. Don't forget to wash them before you eat, too. Soap cleans germs off of your skin, and toothpaste gets rid of germs on your teeth. A scratch or scrape may need a disinfectant to kill germs.

Your body needs exercise! Keep fit by being active, playing sports regularly, and enjoying the fresh air outdoors. Your machine must be kept running or it will start to rust!

Try always to have good posture.

Eat all sorts of different foods! Not too much, not too little, but eat a variety every day. A good breakfast is a good start to the day. Your body needs a boost of energy after several hours without food. One of the great tragedies of our time is that, in certain parts of the world, thousands of people die of malnutrition every year. Weakened by lack of proper food, their bodies aren't strong enough to fight off disease and infection.

Make sure you have enough sleep. You must give your body time to rest if it is to grow up healthy and strong. Don't go to bed too late—an hour's sleep before midnight is worth two afterward!

Regular checkups
Like an engine, your body needs a checkup from time to time. Your doctor will make sure all is well.

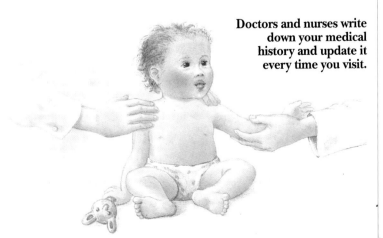

Doctors and nurses write down your medical history and update it every time you visit.

Babies grow and change so quickly that they need to see a doctor several times in their first year. They should have a series of vaccinations before the age of two. Older children need boosters to keep the vaccinations up to date. A dentist should check and clean your teeth twice a year.

All the medical checks in the world are not enough, though, if you don't try to know your own body and look after your health!

The rhythms of life

Each person's body has a built-in rhythm, which follows the course of day and night and the seasons, warm or cold. Some people are more active in the evening and like to get up late. Others are early birds and prefer to go to bed early too. Some people work all night long, like nurses and shift workers in factories. Their internal clocks have to adjust to different rhythms.

Animals and plants have their rhythms too.

A cat can sleep just as well during the day as at night. Many wild animals are constantly on guard against their enemies and only get snatches of sleep—giraffes sleep for only 10 minutes at a time! But monkeys and birds may sleep for 12 hours or more high in the tops of tall trees.

The life of a plant follows the rhythm of light and dark. Daisies, tulips, and water lilies keep their petals shut until daybreak.

Everyone has a built-in clock. It regulates how your body works. At night, though, you don't simply switch off; many things go on as you sleep. Large amounts of growth hormone are produced to help repair or replace damaged tissue. Your body temperature is lower in the morning; it rises with all the activities of the day. When you travel to a place in a different time zone, it takes a few days for your internal clock to catch up to your watch.

Following the rhythms of the seasons
Some animals spend the winter asleep. If you live in a cold climate, you might like to as well—it's hard to get up on those cold, dark mornings. In the spring, the warmer weather lifts your spirits and seems to give you new energy. The summer sunshine builds your body's supply of vitamin D, which you will need to help you through the winter. In autumn, nature slows down. But it's back to school for you, perhaps with a new teacher and a new class.

Intriguing facts, activities, games, a quiz, and a glossary, followed by the index

Different ways to celebrate a baby's birth

In certain countries, people bake special bread and decorate it to look like a little baby. Sometimes they make the loaf in the shape of the placenta, as a reminder of how the baby was fed until it was born.

In some parts of Africa,

the placenta from child-birth is buried in the ground and a tree is planted over it. The tree belongs to the child, who can watch it grow as he or she grows older from year to year.

In countries with hot climates, babies and children don't need to wear very many clothes.

A baby can sleep in all sorts of places!

Amazonian Indians in South America put their babies in hammocks, and they sleep hanging above the ground. They are safely out of the way of any crawling insects that might give them a nasty bite.

This Chinese baby is sleeping soundly in a hammock made of cloth.

In parts of Mongolia, babies sleep on the carpet in the big family tent.

Western babies often sleep in bassinets that rock or swing, just as they did long ago.

In rural Japan, parents may take their babies to work in the fields with them, tucked up in a cozy basket.

Long ago, babies used to be wrapped up snugly in wide bandages called swaddling bands.

If a mother could not feed her baby, she would hire a "wet nurse" who would breast feed that baby as well as her own.

A new-born baby in the 12th century   Roman baby

The first bottles for

babies were invented in the 18th century. They were simply horns filled with cows' milk.

A baby around 1900

About 1850, babies began to be dressed in long, wide dresses so that they could kick their legs.

Today, babies can be as active as they like. They are soon dressed like the rest of the family.

■ Did you know?

In the Middle Ages, few people had beds. The whole family slept on the same mattress, which was made of straw or leaves.

Up until the 18th century, children slept in their parents' bed. Later they shared a bed with their brothers and sisters.

A country-style box bed

Toward the middle of the 18th century, people built their houses with a new room: the bedroom, separate from the living rooms. Also, beds became narrower.

Only during the past 100 years or so have children slept one to a bed, and only recently have they been given a bedroom of their own.

The Japanese sleep on a mattress called a futon, which is rolled away during the day.

Every country has its own customs. There are many different ways to go to bed.

Lapplanders sleep on a mattress of branches, covered with reindeer hide.

In Morocco, some people sleep wrapped in a blanket on the carpet of their tent.

Pygmies lay out sleeping mats on a raised platform safely above the insects on the ground!

In India, people sometimes bring their beds out onto the pavement when it's hot.

When they are on the move, Tibetans go to sleep simply wrapped up in blankets.

Beds from the past

Long ago, beds were highly decorated.

An Egyptian bed

A four-poster bed in the classical style

Polish bed, 18th century

Raised, boat-shaped bed of the 1800s

Bed of State

Bed shaped like a swan, French, mid-19th century

Western beds are made up of a base with a mattress on top.

Have you ever slept in a bunk bed like this one?

Who do you look like?

When a baby is born, everyone tries to see who he or she looks like! You inherit features from your parents: skin shade, eye and hair color, the shape of your face, your voice, and even your talents and shortcomings. It's called heredity. These special characteristics are passed on through your genes. Are you like your father or mother, your uncle or aunt, a grandparent?

Look at the color of other peoples' eyes.

Brown eyes are far more common worldwide than blue eyes. See how some eyes have several different shades of color.

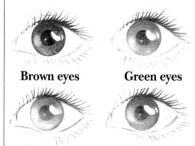

Brown eyes **Green eyes**

Grey eyes **Blue eyes**

Look at the members of your family. In what way do they look alike, and how are they different? Don't forget that features come through your father and your mother, who have inherited genes from their parents, so your nose may be like your grand-mother's! You even inherited the character of your tongue—some can roll their tongue, others can't.

Can you?

Can you believe your eyes?
Sometimes your brain is deceived by what your eyes have seen. Optical illusions give you false information, so that your brain can't interpret the image correctly.

1. Do these two shapes look the same to you?
Trace over one, then lay the tracing over the other shape. Does it fit?

2. Are the vertical lines parallel?
Yes, they are.

3. Which of these figures is taller?
Use a ruler to check. Were you surprised by the answer?

4. Are the smaller squares below all the same size?
Yes, they are.

5. Stare at these black squares for a moment.
You will see gray dots appear where the lines intersect. If you move the paper away a little, the spots will be even more noticeable.

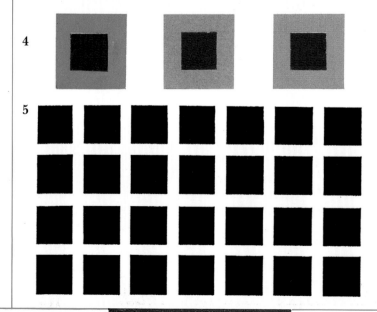

Fingerprints
Everybody's fingerprints are different.

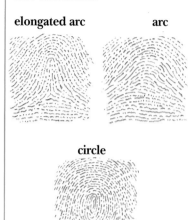

elongated arc **arc**

circle

spiral **loop**

To take a fingerprint, rub a spot on a piece of paper with a soft pencil until it's black. Press your finger onto the black spot. Put a piece of clear tape over your blackened fingertip, peel back the tape and press it onto some white paper. Now see what kind of fingerprint you have.

Even identical twins can often have different fingerprints.

What shape are the lobes of your ears?

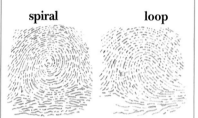 

attached **detached**

Some people can't tell the difference between the colors red and green, or more rarely, blue. They are colorblind.

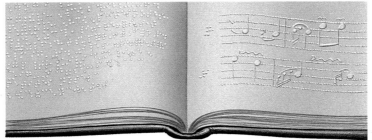

The Braille alphabet
People with poor sight or no sight at all can't read an ordinary book. Louis Braille, a Frenchman who was blind, invented an alphabet using a system of six raised dots, which are punched into thick paper. People who are blind can learn to read books written in Braille by running their fingertips over the pages. They can also read music in this way.

The animal with the largest eyes is the giant squid. Its eyes are nearly 15 inches (38 cm) in diameter!

The male silkworm has thousands of tiny scent organs on its antennae to help it pick up smells.

Caterpillars are covered with hairs that react to sound. They can freeze at the slightest noise.

Chameleons can look in two directions at the same time. Their eyes swivel around independently of each other.

Is it possible to transplant an eye? No, you can't replace a whole eye, but you can transplant a cornea. Today it's a simple operation that has saved many people's sight.

Tarsier

Chameleon

The small tarsier, a nocturnal animal related to the lemur, has the largest eyes in proportion to its size of any mammal.

■ How do doctors examine your heart?

They can listen to your heartbeat with a stethoscope.

An electrocardiogram (EKG) displays patterns of impulses, which show in more detail how healthy the heart is.

If a heart isn't working properly, or a baby is born with a heart defect, the doctor may treat the problem with drugs or correct it with surgery.

Occasionally, the only way to save a patient's life is with a heart transplant. In a long and extremely delicate operation, the doctor removes the diseased heart and puts a healthy heart, taken from someone who has just died, in its place.

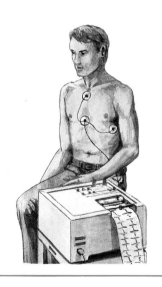

■ Did you know?

In cases of severe burns, skin tissues have been so badly damaged that they are no longer able to heal on their own. Doctors perform a skin graft; a thin strip of skin is lifted from a healthy part of the patient's body, and stuck, or grafted, onto the injury to help the wound to heal.

Some people do not have any pigments at all— their hair is white, their eyes are pink, and their skin is pale. They are albinos. This is very rare in humans, but occurs more often in animals. You may have seen an albino rabbit or a mouse with white fur and pink eyes.

There are many variations in the color of skin, from darkest black to freckled white. Whatever its shade, skin is always colored by the same pigment, called melanin.

In pale skin, melanin is concentrated in one small space in each skin cell. In dark skin, melanin spreads out, darkening the whole cell. The color of a person's skin does not depend on the amount of melanin, but on how widely it is distributed.

Germs don't have to be harmful. Sometimes, tanker ships carrying oil (for our cars and homes) spill some of their cargo, polluting the water and harming wildlife. But now, scientists have developed dried bacteria which activate in water and literally eat the oil spills. One pound of the bacteria can hold almost two gallons (8 l) of oil! The bacteria are living things, and do not harm the environment that they are used to clean.

Rhythms of the heart

A baby's heartbeat is fast at birth; it beats 140 times per minute. An adult's resting heartbeat is about 75 times a minute. The rhythm speeds up when you exercise. It isn't good for your heart to beat either too fast or too slowly. It beats faster when you have a temperature.

If you're frightened, your heart can stop for a split second and then start again; it has literally "skipped a beat."

Human ears can't pick up every sound. Some noises you hear are higher pitched than others.

The higher the sound, the more sound wave vibrations it gives out each second. The sound waves are measured in units called Hertz, or Hz for short.

Sounds below 20 Hz are too low for humans to hear; these sounds are called infra-sounds.

The human voice has a range of between 200 and 4,000 Hz. Like a cat, a newborn baby can hear sounds of up to 30,000 Hz. A child can hear up to 20,000 Hz, an adult of 30, up to 16,000 Hz, a 50-year-old adult, up to 8,000 Hz, and a person of 80, just 4,000 Hz. Sounds above 20,000 Hz are called ultrasounds.

Dogs can hear sounds up to 40,000 Hz. But the ultrasound champions are dolphins and bats— they can hear up to 150,000 Hz!

Opossums fall into a trance, hypnotized by the swaying of a snake.

A different kind of sleep

Hypnosis is a type of sleep brought about by a special use of words and gestures or sounds. People who are hypnotized look as though they are asleep, but they can still hear and obey orders. Some animals have the power to hypnotize. Their prey is so fascinated by their movements that the prey is unable to move, until suddenly the killer springs. A mongoose can hypnotize and kill a snake in this way.

People who are hearing impaired often use sign language to communicate. Sign language is made up of hand movements, which people can make rapidly and understand in an instant. People who are hearing impaired also become good at lip reading. Highly sophisticated hearing aids can help some people pick up certain sounds.

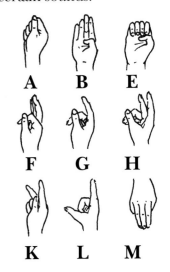

Some mind-altering drugs come from plants, and others are chemically produced. These drugs act on neurons, the nerve cells that link every part of the body to the brain. Gradually, drugs destroy a person's neurons, even if they are not aware of the damage being done. Once a neuron is destroyed, it is gone for good. Neurons can never be replaced!

■ Quiz

Can you answer these questions? The correct answers are on the bottom of page 71.

1. While a baby is inside its mother, the umbilical cord helps it
a. stay in place.
b. get nutrients.
c. develop its muscles.

2. Which of these organs only starts to work once a baby is born?
a. the heart
b. the brain
c. the lungs

3. A baby begins to hear
a. when he's in the womb.
b. when he's born.
c. a few days after birth.

4. How many genes does a human being have?
a. about 50,000
b. more than 10 million
c. 23 pairs

5. As your heart pumps, oxygenated blood and stale blood
a. sometimes mix.
b. never mix.
c. mix all the time.

6. Your sense of balance is found in your
a. brain.
b. ears.
c. legs.

7. Which organ in your body needs germs to help it work properly?
a. the brain
b. the heart
c. the intestine

8. The word "virus" means
a. poison.
b. vein.
c. tiny.

9. The smallest bones in the body are located
a. in the hands.
b. in the mouth.
c. in the ears.

10. The size of the pupil in the center of the eye varies depending on
a. your age.
b. what you are thinking about.
c. the amount of light.

11. Because you have two eyes, you are able to see things
a. in detail.
b. from both sides at once.
c. in three dimensions.

12. If you can see close-up things clearly, but not distant things, you are
a. nearsighted.
b. farsighted.
c. colorblind.

True or false?

1. Antibodies are a type of virus.

2. Not eating breakfast in the morning is a good way to lose weight.

3. All vitamins can be made in the body.

4. Genes are passed onto you from both your mother and father.

5. The study of similarities between parents and children is called genetic science.

6. Laid end to end, all the blood vessels in your body would measure about 93,000 miles.

7. Antibiotics kill bacteria and viruses.

8. The gender of a baby is decided the moment the egg is fertilized.

9. The two sides of your heart are separate from each other.

10. Veins leave your heart and arteries return to it.

11. Blood cells are made in your bone marrow.

12. When you are asleep, your brain is resting too.

■ Do you know the answers to these questions?

1. What did artist Leonardo da Vinci, composer Ludwig van Beethoven, and actor Charlie Chaplin have in common?

They were all left-handed.

2. If you are "ambidextrous," what can you do?

Use both your right and left hands equally well.

3. How tall are African pygmies?

They are the smallest race of people in the world. None of them is taller than five feet.

Answers:

Quiz
1 b, 2 c, 3 a, 4 a, 5 b, 6 b, 7 c, 8 a, 9 c, 10 c, 11 c, 12 a.

True or false
1. False (antibodies are substances made by the body to help fight off disease), 2. False (your body needs energy in the morning, because it has had no fuel for 12 hours), 3. False (vitamins come from food. Only vitamin D is produced in the body), 4. True, 5. True, 6. True (nearly four times around Earth), 7. False (only bacteria), 8. True, 9. True, 10. False (it's the opposite), 11. True, 12. False (your brain is active, sorting out the events of the day and dreaming).

■ Glossary

Abdomen: the part of the body between the chest and hips.

AIDS: a serious illness caused by the HIV virus. It attacks the body's defense systems, making people unable to fight off diseases. Presently AIDS is

incurable, but researchers are finding ways to extend infected people's lives. The virus is transmitted mainly through sexual contact and sharing needles with an infected drug user.

Allergy: a reaction, such as a runny nose, a rash, or wheezing, suffered by people sensitive to certain substances, foods, or even medicines. At least one person in 10 has allergy symptoms occasionally.

Anesthetic: a substance that takes away a patient's sensitivity to pain. A general anesthetic puts you to sleep before an operation. An anesthetist is the doctor in charge of keeping you in this state of artificial sleep. A local anesthetic simply numbs a small area for a short time, so that a wound can be stitched up, for example. Dentists give you a local anesthetic when they have to drill a tooth.

Antibiotics: drugs that can kill bacteria, stopping them from growing or from reproducing. They do not kill viruses and so cannot cure viral diseases such as colds or flus. Penicillin is still the most commonly used antibiotic.

Booster: a second dose of a vaccine, given at a later date to increase the amount of antibodies and give extra protection. School-age children are given a booster of some of the vaccines they were given as babies.

Cartilage: soft, elastic white tissue that covers the ends of bones at the joints. It's also found in your nose and ear lobes.

Cholesterol: a fatty substance found in foods like egg yolks and shellfish. A high level of cholesterol in the blood can lead to hardening of the arteries and heart disease, particularly in men.

Constipation: if your intestines cannot get rid of undigested food, because of lack of fiber (roughage) or water in your diet, this solid waste matter becomes hard and dry. You are constipated. It's difficult to have a bowel movement, and you may get a stomachache.

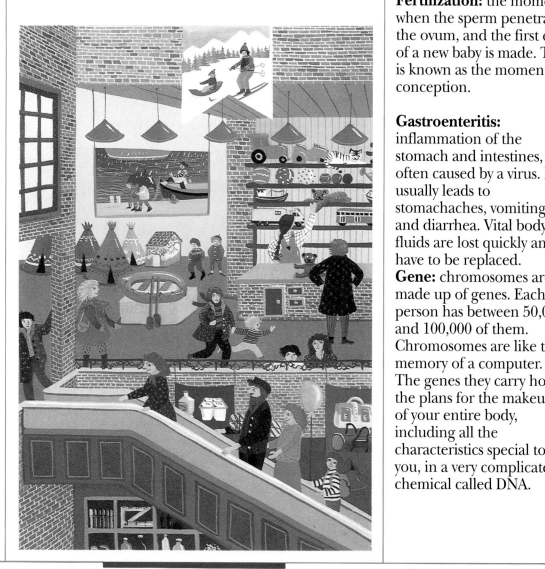

Diagnose: to discover what disease someone has from looking at their symptoms and sometimes carrying out tests. Doctors must make accurate diagnoses in order to treat patients successfully.

Fertilization: the moment when the sperm penetrates the ovum, and the first cell of a new baby is made. This is known as the moment of conception.

Gastroenteritis: inflammation of the stomach and intestines, often caused by a virus. It usually leads to stomachaches, vomiting, and diarrhea. Vital body fluids are lost quickly and have to be replaced.

Gene: chromosomes are made up of genes. Each person has between 50,000 and 100,000 of them. Chromosomes are like the memory of a computer. The genes they carry hold the plans for the makeup of your entire body, including all the characteristics special to you, in a very complicated chemical called DNA.

Immunity: if you are immune to an illness, your body has built up a stock of antibodies against that illness and you will not become sick. You can become immune to a disease by having vaccinations or by coming into contact with a disease.

Membrane: a thin skin covering organs such as the heart and lungs and lining the nose, mouth, and intestine. Many lining membranes produce mucus, a moistening, lubricating, and protective fluid, and they are then known as mucous membranes.

Menstruation: when a girl reaches puberty, she produces a mature ovum every 28 days or so. The uterus grows a thick lining just in case the egg is fertilized and becomes an embryo. If this doesn't happen, the lining is shed,

along with some blood, down through the vagina. This bleeding is known as a period, or menstruation, and lasts about four or five days in each month.

Nucleus: the central part of a cell; the nucleus contains the chromosomes.

Oxygen: living things could not exist without oxygen, a colorless, odorless gas found in the air you breathe.

Parasite: an animal (or plant) that lives in or on another living thing, taking its food from it.

Penis: one of the male reproductive organs, also used for passing urine out of the body.

Pigment: the substance that gives your skin, hair, and eyes their color.

Pituitary gland: gland at the base of the brain that produces and releases several hormones. These include growth hormones and those that stimulate a man's testes to produce sperm and woman's ovaries to develop egg cells.

Plaque: a harmful film that forms on teeth. Careful brushing, flossing, and regular visits to the dentist can control plaque.

Saliva: fluid produced by glands in the mouth. Saliva moistens food so that it can be swallowed easily and helps to begin the digestion process.

Stethoscope: instrument used by a doctor to hear what is going on inside a person's body.

Tissues: groups of similar cells that are bound together to form various parts of the body—for instance, muscle tissue or nerve tissue.

Vaccination: an injection of a small dose of a weakened or dead bacteria or virus. This stimulates the body's natural defense system to produce antibodies against the disease. Vaccinations are one way humans can be protected from certain illnesses.

Vagina: the passageway from the uterus to the outside of a girl's body. It is made of muscle lined with membrane. During childbirth, the vagina stretches as the baby exits the womb.

Virus: a type of germ that causes infectious diseases.

Viruses can cause measles, chicken pox, colds, and sore throats.

Warm-blooded: keeping the same inside body temperature regardless of the outside temperature.

■ Accidents and Emergencies

Accidents and emergencies happen very quickly and without warning. It might be that the person who needs our help can't even talk. What can you do to help?

Tell the person who is hurt to stay still while you get an adult to help you. Call out for help if there are people nearby. If there is no adult nearby, go to the nearest phone and dial 911. This call is free, even from a pay phone. Try to remain calm. Tell them your name, where you are, and what happened. The operator who answers will tell you what you can do until help arrives.

Always remember, when someone is hurt you must make sure that you are in no danger yourself. You must not go near if there is any risk that you will be injured. It is better to get help. Don't try to move an injured person. You could possibly hurt the person even more by moving him or her.

In an emergency
Call out for help or get an adult to help you.
Call 911.
Cover the person with a blanket.

Fainting

People faint for many different reasons. Someone may faint if he or she gets very hot or has a bad shock. People who faint usually recover within a few minutes. Lift their legs about eight to 12 inches (20 to 30 cm) off the ground; that is about the distance from your elbow to the tips of your fingers. If you think they may have been hurt in a fall, it is best not to move them.

Strains and sprains

It hurts when a person twists an ankle, overstretches a muscle, or wrenches a joint. The pain is probably a sign that they have a strain or sprain. Many people treat sprains and strains at home. If the following four things are true, they most likely have a sprain or strain, and not something more serious: 1. The person is able to move the hurt area; 2. There is only a small amount of bruising; 3. It does not hurt when the person rests it; and 4. It does not tingle or feel numb.

The person should rest the injured area and call a doctor or check a first aid handbook to find out how to treat the injury.

Broken bones

If someone has been knocked down, has fallen heavily, or has been in an accident, he or she may have broken a bone. The hurt area will be painful and may be an unusual shape. The person may not be able to move it, and it may be cold, blue, or numb. Tell the person not to move. Hold the injured limb above and below the suspected break, to support it and keep it still.

Burns and scalds

If someone burns or scalds themselves, you must cool the burnt area by putting it in cold water until the pain has gone. If a person's clothes catch fire, tell the person to stop, drop to the ground, and roll to put out the flames.

First aid training

First aid training teaches you how to help someone who is ill or injured. The Red Cross offers First aid courses in communities everywhere. To find out about classes, ask at your school or your local library, or contact your local chapter of the Red Cross.

■ **What can you do to stay safe and healthy? Here are some important tips:**

For your health

1. Wash your hands frequently, especially before eating and after using the toilet.
2. Get plenty of exercise.
3. Drink eight to 10 glasses of water every day.
4. Eat a variety of healthy foods.

Safety at home

1. Ask your parents or guardian to keep these emergency numbers by the telephone:
   Ambulance: 911 or _____
   Poison Control Center: _____
   Fire Department: 911 or: _____
   Police: 911 or _____
   Doctor: _____
   Hospital: _____
2. Keep your address and phone number by the telephone. In an emergency, you may forget them.
3. Practice a fire exit plan with your family.
4. Never play with guns, whether they are loaded or not.

Safety when you're out

1. Always use a seat belt when you are riding in the car.
2. Wear a helmet when you are riding your bicycle, skating, or skiing.
3. Learn the rules of the road for bicycling and walking. Contact your school or library to find out about classes and books.
4. Never go anywhere with someone you don't know unless your parents or guardian say it's all right.

The entries in **bold** refer to whole chapters on the subject.